Risk

Adversaries
and Allies

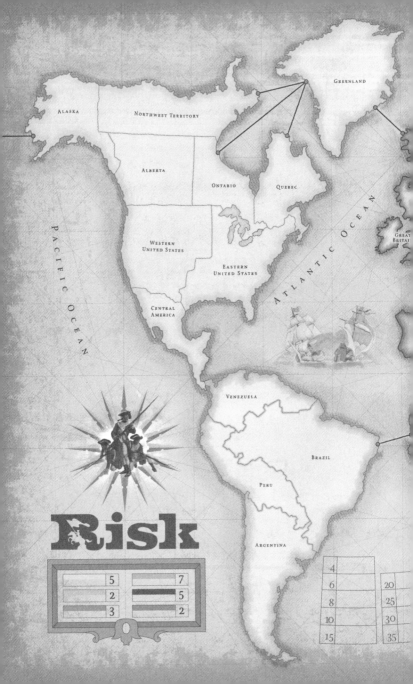

Risk

Adversaries and Allies

MASTERING STRATEGIC RELATIONSHIPS

ALAN AXELROD

STERLING

New York / London
www.sterlingpublishing.com

STERLING and the distinctive Sterling logo are registered trademarks of
Sterling Publishing Co., Inc.

HASBRO and its logo and RISK are trademarks of Hasbro and are used
with permission. © 2008 Hasbro. All rights reserved.

Library of Congress Cataloging-in-Publication Data
Axelrod, Alan, 1952-
  Risk : adversaries and allies : mastering strategic relationships /
Alan Axelrod.
      p. cm.
  Includes bibliographical references and index.
  ISBN 978-1-4027-5411-1
  1. Strategic planning--Case studies. 2. International relations--
Risk assessment--Case studies. 3. Strategic alliances (Business)--
Case studies. 4. Risk (Game) I. Title.
  HD30.28.A98 2009
  658'.044--dc22

                                                        2008046873

10   9   8   7   6   5   4   3   2   1

Published by Sterling Publishing Co., Inc.
387 Park Avenue South, New York, NY 10016
© 2009 by Alan Axelrod
Distributed in Canada by Sterling Publishing
c/o Canadian Manda Group, 165 Dufferin Street
Toronto, Ontario, Canada M6K 3H6
Distributed in the United Kingdom by GMC Distribution Services
Castle Place, 166 High Street, Lewes, East Sussex, England BN7 1XU
Distributed in Australia by Capricorn Link (Australia) Pty. Ltd.
P.O. Box 704, Windsor, NSW 2756, Australia

Book design and layout: Sherry Williams/Oxygen Design
Please see picture credits page for image credits.

Manufactured in the United States of America
All rights reserved

Sterling ISBN 978-1-4027-5411-1

For information about custom editions, special sales, premium and
corporate purchases, please contact Sterling Special Sales
Department at 800-805-5489 or specialsales@sterlingpublishing.com.

CONTENTS

INTRODUCTION

RISK
as a Model for Modern Decision Makers

ARTHUR CONOLLY WAS A MAN of many guises. An explorer and writer, he was also a captain of the Anglo-Indian 6th Bengal Light Cavalry, but functioned more immediately in the employ of the British East India Company as a spy. Intrepid and bold, he took espionage seriously, yet also with a sufficient sense of humor to travel incognito throughout Central Asia under the name Khan Ali, a Middle Eastern play on his distinctly Western surname. Writing in 1829 to Sir Henry Rawlinson, another man of many works—soldier, diplomat, and gentleman-scholar of ancient Persian texts—Conolly coined the term the "Great Game" as a label for the diplomatic contest between the British and Russian empires for political control over Central Asia.

For Conolly, the Great Game ended in June 1842 when Nasrullah Khan, the emir of Bukhara, executed him as a British spy. But his phrase lived on. Historians came to use it to describe the intense period of diplomatic maneuvering between the two empires spanning roughly 1813 to 1907, but it was also applied to global diplomacy more generally thereafter, up to the period of World War II.

Following that world-consuming conflict, some historians recognized the start of the "New Great Game," a label they bestowed on the Cold War jockeying for global dominance—no longer between the British and the Russians, but between the Americans and the Soviets.

If strategy is an overall plan for accomplishing some goal—whether the strategy is produced by and applied to a single person, a business enterprise, or an entire nation—diplomacy is the omnibus term for all the means, moral or immoral, peaceful or warlike, used to engage with other people, enterprises, or nations to get what you, your enterprise, or your nation wants. Whatever the scale involved—individual, corporate, or national—diplomacy is deadly serious, with everything at stake. Yet Conolly and many others after him saw it all as a game.

Cynical? Shocking? Or just a little backwards? We are, after all, accustomed to children imitating "real life" in the games they play. The surprise is that real life—serious and consequential though it assuredly is—can often imitate a game. The perception, or perhaps the realization, that the relationship between games and life is not one way, but interchangeable in direction, is behind the current interest in game theory among politicians, diplomats, military heads, and business leaders.

Once you accept the two-way flow of game into life and life into game, the notion of a "Great Game" no longer seems so shocking, cynical, irreverent, or trivial. Only consider that game theory was born in 1944 when the eminent mathematician John von Neumann teamed up with the economist Oskar Morgenstern to write *Theory of Games and Economic Behavior*, which soon became the basic textbook that the legendary Cold War–era think tank, the RAND Corporation, used to develop the scenarios and strategies that formed the basis of America's nuclear weapons policy. In the Atomic Age, playing at diplomacy became playing at doomsday. And, strange as it sounds, that was a good thing, since it is far better to play at doomsday than actually to implement it.

Whether applied to global thermonuclear war, Cold War diplomacy, current diplomacy, strategies for big businesses and small, or to individual decision making, game theory is a means of modeling and studying strategic interactions between players (or "agents"—the people who make decisions and take actions). It is fundamental to game theory that players choose strategies they believe will maximize their return, always in the context of the strategies chosen by the *other* players of the game. Game theory assumes that, in "social situations" (situations that may be on the scale of just two or three individuals, the entire planet, or somewhere in between), people ("agents," "CEOs," "national leaders," "generals," call them what you will) likewise attempt to embrace strategies of optimization.

In other words, everyone tries to win.

And since everyone in a given social situation is trying to win, the strategies they choose interact, compete, conflict, cooperate, succeed, and fail, always in relation to one another. There are many variables that make the study of comparative strategy in social situations both fascinating and, typically, desperately complex. For example, human variables include rationality, irrationality, genius, wisdom, skill, mediocrity, incompetence, misperception, idiocy, and the like. Natural variables may encompass climate, weather, topography, and population. Add to this a handful of random variables, including luck, chance, destiny, and Divine Providence.

Because the real world presents so many variables, modeling strategy within the far simpler spatial and temporal confines of a game can be a very valuable way of understanding and evaluating different strategies, pitting one against another. Equally important is the fact that it is almost always far more economical to "game out" a personal life choice, a business strategy, or a proposed national policy than it is to jump into, say, a marriage, launch a new product line, or invade a nation—all for real— and simply hope for the best.

Game theorists have used many different games to model the reality of social situations, ranging from the most basic—simple card and dice games—to the most ancient—chess and go, for example—to more modern games. (My own *Everything I Know about Business I Learned from Monopoly* was published in 2002.) But no contemporary game holds greater interest and more potential for game theory—for modeling real-world strategy— than RISK.

The game was originally the brainchild of Albert Lamorisse, best known to film buffs as the writer, director, and producer of the classic 1956 French short film *The Red Balloon,* but immortalized among game enthusiasts as the creator of "La Conquête du Monde"— World Conquest—a board game published in France in 1957 by a company called Miro. That same year, Miro approached the American game-making giant Parker

Brothers, which purchased "La Conquête," made some revisions to the basic rules, and in 1959 brought out "Risk: The Continental Game." Some believe the new name was a stroke of genius. Others say that it represented nothing more than the initials of the four grandchildren of the Parker Brothers executive in charge of marketing the game. In either case, the RISK title was soon tweaked a final time as "RISK: THE GAME OF GLOBAL DOMINATION."

Since its introduction, RISK has appeared in various additional versions. There have been *Castle Risk* (1986), *Risk: Édition Napoléon* (1999), *Risk: Édition Napoléon: Extension Empire Ottoman* (2000), *Risk: 2210 A.D.* (2001), *Risk: The Lord of the Rings* (2002), *Risk: The Lord of the Rings: Gondor & Mordor Expansion Set* (2003), *Risk: The Lord of the Rings: Trilogy Edition* (2003), *Risk: Godstorm* (2004), *Risk: Star Wars: Clone Wars Edition*, *Risk: Star Wars Original Trilogy Edition* (2006), *Risk Junior: Narnia* (2006), and *Risk: The Transformers Edition* (2007), which is based on the *Transformers* blockbuster movie. In addition to the board versions of the game, there are computer-based and online formats. Parker Brothers and Avalon Hill, which publish the various versions of the game, are now divisions of Hasbro.

In its original form and format, RISK is played by two to six players, one of whom survives to the end of the game and is therefore the winner: the player who has conquered the world. There are no ties and no ambiguities. At the end of the game, the sole conqueror remains. Every token on the board is the same color and belongs to the victor.

The RISK game board is a simplified world map divided into 42 territories, and the game comes with six sets of armies, each of a different color, with each set consisting of infantry, cavalry, and artillery pieces. There are also five dice, which are used to determine the outcome of attacks and defenses, and cards, which are collected as a player conquers territories and which are used to secure reinforcements to the player's army. The object of the game is simple: to win by conquering the world. This means acquiring territories and continents by using one's army tokens to occupy unoccupied territories and by successfully invading territories held by others, yet without leaving oneself vulnerable to invasion and conquest in return. In each of the game's many turns—and games often assume marathon proportions—each player must decide whether to attack, where to attack, when to attack, and when to stop attacking.

That is the game in a proverbial nutshell. But because this description leaves unanswered the question of why RISK is so interesting to game theorists who want to model the real world realistically, we need to push the discussion a bit further.

Unlike chess, which models decision making on a highly logical, even quasi-mathematical level, requiring the ideal player to think strictly in terms of perfect moves, RISK provides a multiplicity of winning (and losing!) options with every turn in each game. There is no one right or wrong strategy. There is no one right or wrong move. Strategic and tactical choices alike offer a whole range of benefits and liabilities.

In RISK, spatial strategy is important—placing pieces for effective occupation, conquest, defense, and movement from one territory to another—but so is the ability to envision, formulate, and execute genuine negotiations with other players. As in poker played at the highest of levels, a capacity to "read" others, to see the game from their perspective, to get into their heads, to manipulate them, to cajole them, to persuade them, and even to deceive them, is critically important to victory. Yet also as in poker—and in contrast to chess—chance plays a significant role, just as it does in real life. The winning player cannot rely solely on chance, of course, but must always factor it into strategy and style of play.

This book, like its companions in the RISK series, is not a how-to manual for winning RISK, and you don't even need to play RISK to enjoy and benefit from the book. In fact, we won't even be talking specifically about the game of RISK in the rest of the book. The chapters that follow are devoted instead to some of the most significant—that is, momentous and instructive—strategic decisions in history: the game of "real life." And that game gets you deep into the same issues RISK offers in model form only:

- A competition for limited resources

- The absolute necessity of making decisions

- The necessity—if you hope to win—of making strategic decisions

- The ever-present potential for conflict

- The ever-present potential for the resolution of conflict through war or diplomacy

- The need to define, create, and end relationships, including alliances and enmities

- The need to influence, persuade, dissuade, intimidate, force, and cooperate with others

- The necessity for managing time and timing

- And the urgent requirement that chance be accepted, managed, exploited, coped with, and compensated for

As a rich example of game theory, RISK is neither more nor less than a stunningly useful way to start thinking clearly about strategic decision making in the real world—the game board on which the chapters of this book will be played out. The object? To learn to make the moves that will win the greatest "Great Game" of them all: *your* profession, *your* passion, *your* life.

CHAPTER 1

The Limits of Loyalty

A Pragmatic Approach to Alliance and Enmity

Previous page: *RISK game board.*

The Limits of Loyalty

EVERY INDIVIDUAL AND EVERY ENTERPRISE make alliances. Some are formal, solemnized by contracts, letters of agreements, and treaties, but even more of them are informal, established by verbal understandings, or simply taken more or less for granted, as when we turn to a family member or close friend for help. All but the most rudimentary of human activities depends on alliances. Civilization is built on them. In his 1937 novel *To Have and Have Not,* Ernest Hemingway has his dying hero Harry Morgan stammer out the situation as bluntly as it has ever been put: "'A man,' Harry Morgan said, looking at them both. 'One man alone ain't got. No man alone now.' He stopped. 'No matter how a man alone ain't got no bloody fucking chance.'"

Virtually everything we do in life is collaborative. That is the indispensable benefit of alliances. But, as with most tactical and strategic necessities, the potential benefits are balanced by potential risk. If we gain by collaboration, we may lose by betrayal. As illustrated in Chapter 5, this was the lesson Joseph Stalin learned—on the largest and most horrific scale possible—from his short-lived alliance with Adolf Hitler. Yet, without making tactical alliances (alliances to accomplish some short-term, immediate objective) and strategic alliances (those created to attain a long-term, overall goal), you cannot exert much influence in your world—whether that world is bounded by the four walls of an office or encompasses the entire planet—without using the threat of force or force itself. Since few of us command sufficient force to bully our way through life, and since at least some of us would have moral reservations about exercising that force even if we could, it is almost always advantageous to forge alliances rather than remain neutral or attempt to go it alone.

The calculus of risk and reward in any alliance depends on the allies involved, their goals individually and collectively, their resources (again, individually and collectively), and the situation at hand; however, in general, despite the possibility of outright betrayal, alliances offer more benefits than liabilities. If your ally prevails, you benefit from his victory. This holds true whether you are weaker, stronger, or equally matched with him. If you happen to be more powerful than your ally, he will answer to you, and if your ally is stronger than you, she will feel obliged to you for whatever aid and support you are able to render her. Even if you and your ally lose in a given exchange, all is not lost. You still have an ally. Although, then, any alliance is better than no alliance, there is always an advantage in the weaker, less powerful, less influential partner allying to a stronger, more powerful, more influential one. The benefits of alliance do flow both ways, but they flow far more abundantly and rapidly downhill, from the greater to the lesser partner.

Alliances can be crafted in many variations and degrees, but, generally speaking, they fall into one of two categories.

An *absolute alliance* is, in effect, a bond of honor, friendship, or even kinship. Such an alliance is an attempt at a universal and permanent collaboration under any and all circumstances. Put in diplomatic terms, it is the equivalent of a no-strings-attached military treaty. Country A agrees never under any circumstances to attack Country B. Furthermore, if Country B is attacked by anyone under any circumstance, Country A will automatically and always come to its aid. The famous Monroe Doctrine of December 2, 1823, is an example of an absolute alliance. President James Monroe warned the empires of Europe that the United States would regard any aggression against any of the newly independent nations of the Americas as an attack on the United States—always and under all circumstances.

The advantage of an absolute alliance is a high degree of reliability, which makes for enhanced security and a certain ease when it comes to long-term strategic planning. The disadvantage of this category of alliance is its lack of flexibility. Absolute alliances hem you in, limiting the extent of any alliances you might want to make with others. In some cases, those who are outside of the alliance may perceive you and your ally as inherently hostile to themselves and all others. *Absolute alliances are never used in the game of RISK—after all, there can only be one winner— and they are almost never used in the real world, either.* In business or in global politics, corporations and countries almost always negotiate *limited alliances*. These are typically defined by contracts or treaties that apply to a specific issue or issues or circumstances. They are often additionally limited by time, with, perhaps, options for renewal. Limited alliances give everyone involved in them a lot more flexibility and room for movement than absolute alliances do, but at the cost of long-term stability.

In the end, of course, alliances are concluded mutually; however, they are almost always first proposed by one party or another. In general, you are in the stronger negotiating position when you are approached with a proposal rather than when you initiate the proposal. There are two reasons for this. First, when you are approached, you automatically know that the other party wants or needs something. That puts you in a position of strength as someone who has the power to address the want or need of another. Second, by the very act of approaching you, the other party has already given you something valuable—information. You have come into possession of some knowledge of what the other person wants or needs and what he is willing to give up, to barter, in order to get it. Based on these two advantages, you can respond to the proposal with a counteroffer that, in all likelihood, will get you a greater benefit than if you had made the initial approach.

Of course, you should not jump at every offer of alliance you get. Analyze the cost versus benefit and the risk versus the reward of the proposed alliance. Ask yourself: Do you really need the alliance proposed? What will it give you that you do not already possess? How will it enhance as opposed to limit your prospects? What is the track record of the person, group, or enterprise proposing the alliance? Is it a history of promises kept or of promises broken? Is it a history of advantages bestowed on partners or costs exacted from them? What, finally, is your current relationship with the other party? Are you more naturally competitors or collaborators? Which relationship—ally, adversary, or neutral—is likely to benefit you most?

Creating an alliance is making a deal. Especially in business, there are essentially two kinds of deal makers. There is the man or woman who defines a "good deal" as a victory for him- or herself and a defeat for the other party, and there is the person who sees the best deal as the one from which both (or all) parties derive at least some benefit. These two points of view are analogous to the ruthless salesperson who will claim and promise anything in order to make a sale versus the sales professional who is more interested in creating a customer than in making a particular sale. As the tactics of the first type of salesperson will likely generate a single sale—and maybe one that is quite profitable at that—those of the second type are more likely to forge longer-term customer relationships that will, over time, result in repeated sales. Individually, each of these repeated sales may yield less profit than a single sale made through the ruthless approach, but, taken together, the repeated sales add up to a good deal more and therefore make a more productive contribution to a sustainable business. As every experienced sales professional knows, your best sales prospects are to be found among your current customers. Carrying this analogy back to making an alliance, the best—that is, the most productive and advantageous—alliances are those that endure over time. They do not require the triumph of one party at the expense of the other, but, rather, they result in a collaborative working relationship. A hit-and-run alliance may gain some particular thing—and it may well be something of substantial value—but a genuinely collaborative alliance creates an ongoing enterprise that is greater than the sum of its partners. It creates a synergy that enables the parties involved to do together what they could not do—or could not do as profitably—separately.

Examples of alliances of collaboration that result in impressive synergy include those in Chapters 3, 4, and 8 among the episodes that follow in this book. Strangely enough, however, analyzing successful collaborative alliances tends to lead to a decidedly counterintuitive conclusion. When partners in an alliance obey the dictates of what clearly seems their self-interest—that is, when they act individually in accordance with so-called rational self-interest—they often do not make out as well as when each partner manages to subordinate rational self-interest to the common good or to a collaborative goal. In other words, selfish action is often less productive—even to oneself—than what is to all appearances selfless collaboration. Game theorists—logicians who use games to model real-life decision-making scenarios—illustrate this with something called the "Prisoner's Dilemma": two prisoners are brought before a prosecutor, who tells them—separately—that they can either testify or say nothing. "If you testify against the other person, and he says nothing, you can go free, and the other person will be sentenced to two years. If the other person testifies against you, and you remain silent, he will go free, and you will get two years. If both of you testify against each other, I will make sure that neither of you is sentenced to more than six months. If both of you say nothing, I will keep the two of you in prison for just three months." Individually consulting rational self-interest, what do the prisoners do? Each testifies against the other, aiming to cut his losses in the worst case by risking no more than six months. If, however, they had both rejected rational self-interest and instead acted cooperatively, both agreeing to say nothing, they would have done better, incurring no more than three months each. In most cases, collaboration yields more desirable results for the partners than does the pursuit of obvious rational self-interest.

If there are strong incentives to making alliances, there are equally strong reasons to end them—strategically. In high-stakes work situations, the most successful individuals adopt an attitude that is cooperative, open, courteous, and pleasant. They are not overtly, let alone ostentatiously, competitive. They do not obviously strive to outperform others. They neither exhibit nor incite envy. Instead, they demonstrate loyalty, and they avoid—if at all possible—betraying a partner or stabbing a colleague in the back. This said, the most successful individuals also have a backup plan that includes the intention and the means of retaliating—and doing so decisively—against any partner who backstabs them. They may not initiate the end of an alliance without provocation, but they do respond decisively to terminate it if the other party betrays them. However, the most consistently successful individuals never retaliate from any personal motive of revenge. They do not hold a grudge. As any alliance they make is based on business advantage rather than personal friendship, so the retaliation is never founded on personal vengeance. Both the alliance and its termination in an act of retaliation are means to an end, a way to achieve whatever goal the alliance was intended to attain. Thus the successful individual is often willing to "forgive" the betrayal *after* he has retaliated for it. She does not hold a grudge, but instead invites a resumption of the alliance, provided that she still considers it useful to achieving the desired goal.

The attitude of "forgiveness" implies another lesson to be learned from those who tend to make successful alliances. Such people do not regard any enmity as permanent, nor do they hold any alliance as eternal. They do not confuse dislike or feelings of betrayal with a rational assessment that an alliance is no longer useful. The first is a personal matter, the second a matter of business. Conversely, they are careful to avoid confusing friendship (and the loyalty that goes with friendship) with the ethics of business alliance, in which loyalty lasts as long as an alliance proves productively durable and not a moment longer.

Nor do those who manage alliances successfully always wait until the other party commits an overt act of betrayal or does something else to break the alliance. They end alliances whenever they cease to be productive, for whatever reason that may be and regardless of the wishes of the other party.

The end of an alliance, however, does not automatically mean the beginning of an adversarial or outright hostile relationship. Although there is usually no advantage in remaining generally neutral—maintaining few allies or none at all—there can be significant advantage in redefining the relationship with a particular party from ally to neutral, because it is easier to reactivate an alliance with a neutral party than it is to transform an enemy into a friend.

Alliance and enmity are typically matters of degree, especially in the context of business and commerce. Few alliances are totally successful, and few adversaries are totally hostile. As with any other business tactic or strategy, the productivity of an alliance requires continual monitoring and evaluation, and, also as with any other tactic or strategy, the most reliable, most meaningful measure of effectiveness is expressed in terms of dollars—dollars made, dollars spent, dollars lost as a result of the alliance. This said, the most profitable alliances are synergistic; that is, the sum represented by the alliance exceeds what the allies could achieve individually. This means that, in productive alliances, one party enhances the strengths of the other and/or compensates for the weaknesses of the other. In effect, one takes up at the places where the other leaves off. If, in contrast, the alliance is characterized by frequent duplication of effort, the result is merely multiplication of cost rather than enhanced productivity and profit. Even worse, if the efforts of the allies conflict with one another, the result is waste and destruction. A truly productive alliance is like the operation of a symphony orchestra. The different instruments play different notes and produce different timbres. The result is the expression of a mean-ingful—beautiful—composition. If all the instruments played the same notes and produced the same timbres, they would play together more loudly than any one instru-ment could play individually, but there would be little meaning, interest, or beauty in the result. If the instru-ments were played in opposition to one another, without any attempt at tonal and rhythmic harmony, the result would be a meaningless cacophony.

It is true, that much symphonic music does employ dissonance, instruments deliberately playing at apparent cross-purposes, creating dissonant chords and even purposely producing "wrong" notes. This fact adds an important dimension to our analogy. The most produc-tive alliances are never perfectly harmonious. They not only allow for, but actively encourage disagreement, dispute, and difference of opinion. General George S. Patton Jr. was famous, perhaps infamous, for his insistence on "perfect discipline," which he called "the only kind of discipline." He was emphatic, however, that this did not mean an army intellectually marching in lockstep. "No one is thinking if everyone is thinking alike," he said. Discipline, collaboration, a commitment to cooperation— none of these require intellectual servitude. The most productive alliances are founded on common goals, but the route toward achieving those goals typically includes a lively dialogue, what the early nineteenth-century German philosopher Georg Wilhelm Friedrich Hegel called a *dialectic*, a process of arriving at a goal by proposing a thesis toward it, then developing a contradictory antithesis, and finally resolving the contradiction through a coherent synthesis. Obviously, most alliances don't proceed with such intellectual formality and rigor, but the most productive of them typically incorporate the thesis, antithesis, synthesis progression. The point is that the best partnerships are not based on perfect agreement, let alone duplication of effort. Instead, each partner brings a unique quality into the alliance. Dispute may result and is, in fact, encouraged, because the partners are committed to synthesizing their antithetical positions into a new, useful, productive, profitable whole.

Savvy makers of alliances, we have said, never confuse personal loyalty with the bounds of a business partnership defined strictly by continued usefulness. Nevertheless, basic business ethics demand a certain level of trustworthy, honest conduct. Even the most pragmatic and temporary of alliances must rest on a foundation of trust. This can be a problem, as the iconic Renaissance political philosopher Niccolo Machiavelli recognized. "Trust your enemy," he wrote in *The Prince* (1513), "but don't trust your ally." His point was that you can always rely on your enemy to do something to hurt you—that is, you can safely assume that whatever action your enemy undertakes, its purpose will be transparent: it is intended to do you harm. You cannot, however, trust that everything your ally does is meant for your benefit. Whether in RISK or in the world beyond the game board, an enemy, by definition, cannot betray you; only an ally can. From this, it follows that, just as making alliances can bring substantial benefits (even as they carry substantial risks), so making enemies can bring certain benefits. An enemy—as long as he *is* an enemy—can be trusted to oppose you. This exposes you to danger, of course, but it also sets up your enemy for defeat and exploitation at your hands. Whether in business or on the world stage, the great leaders have always been those skilled at making allies as well as enemies. Just as game theory teaches that those who play to win must be willing to accept the possibility of losing, so those who seek allies must be willing to accept the possibility of making enemies. They are sides of the same coin, both offering the potential of risk and reward.

CHAPTER 2

The Unlikeliest Go-Between

*How Pocahontas Forged an Alliance
That Created America*

∽◦∾

Previous page: *Lithograph of Pocahontas saving Captain John Smith, ca. 1870.*

The Unlikeliest Go-Between

IN A 1962 STUDY, the American literary scholar and critic Philip Young called the story of Pocahontas "one of our few, true native myths." This judgment has the ring of truth about it. After all, who has not heard of Pocahontas? Over the centuries, she and her story have figured in a wide variety of literary and artistic works. The British playwright Ben Jonson, younger rival of William Shakespeare, put Pocahontas in his satirical *Staple of News* in 1625. She was also given prominent coverage in John Davis's highly influential *Travels of Four Years and a Half in the United States of America* (1803) and was the star of such nineteenth-century plays as *The Indian Princess* (James Nelson Barker, 1808), *Pocahontas* (George Washington Parke Custis, 1830), *The Forest Princess* (Charlotte Barnes Conner, 1844), and many more into the early twentieth century. In 1925, the great modernist American poet William Carlos Williams featured Pocahontas in his lyrical historical narrative, *In the American Grain*, and she figures prominently in Hart Crane's twentieth-century American epic poem, *The Bridge* (1930). As Philip Young pointed out, she even foreshadowed and probably inspired many of the heroines created by such classic American writers as Nathaniel Hawthorne, James Fenimore Cooper, and Herman Melville.

Yes, indeed: who has not heard of Pocahontas?

Yet, if asked, how many of us can say just who she was and just what she did?

Those who know her as something more than "some early Indian princess" might relate the story of how she saved the life of one Captain John Smith during the earliest days of Virginia. Born in 1580, Smith was raised on a farm in England at Willoughby near Alford, Lincolnshire, and attended the King Edward VI Grammar School in Louth. Yet after the death of his father, the sixteen-year-old left England for a life at sea and quickly became one of those celebrated Elizabethan "sea dogs": hypermasculine state-sponsored pirates and soldiers of fortune typically featured in stiff portraits of the era, arrayed in high, ruffled collar, shining cuirass—cinched at the waist, broad at the chest—a prominent codpiece, shapely hose, and high, cuffed boots. After a brief career at sea, Smith enlisted as a mercenary in the army of France's Henry IV, fighting against Spain and the Holy League. Next, in the pay of the Austrian Habsburgs, he fought in Hungary against the Ottoman Turks. In 1602, he was wounded in combat, captured, and then sold into slavery. In one of his characteristically self-promotional autobiographical works, *The True Travels, Adventures and Observations of Captain John Smith* (1629), Smith wrote that his Turkish captor sent him as a "gift" to the Turk's beloved, the Lady Charatza Tragabigzanda who, naturally enough (Smith implies), fell in love with him. Smith was taken to the Crimea—either as part of Lady Tragabigzanda's household retinue or as the slave of her brother—from where he managed to escape into Muscovy—modern Russia—and westward into the lands of the Poles and Lithuanians. He variously traveled and soldiered across Europe and into Northern Africa, finally returning to England in 1604.

His fabulous adventures were not unique—not for an Englishman in the age of Elizabeth I and James I—but they did surely mark him as a young man of exceptional courage, daring, resourcefulness, and promise. In 1606 his reputation earned him a position with the Virginia Company of London, which had been granted a royal charter to plant a colony in the vast but vaguely defined American land Sir Walter Raleigh had named Virginia in honor of Elizabeth I, the "Virgin Queen."

So it was that, on December 20, 1606, Captain John Smith figured among the passengers who set sail aboard the *Discovery, Susan Constant,* and *Godspeed,* bound for Virginia. Apparently, neither Captain Christopher Newport, in charge of the flotilla, nor anyone else sailing in those ships knew of Smith's connection with the Virginia Company, and the irascible Smith argued with Newport, repeatedly questioning and defying the captain's orders, making such a nuisance of himself all during the passage that Newport decided to punish him—with nothing less than death by execution—as soon as they should make land. When the ships landed at present-day Cape Henry, Virginia, on April 26, 1607, and before he could get around to dispatching the troublesome Smith, Newport opened the sealed orders he carried from the Virginia Company. Doubtless to his surprise and dismay, he discovered that the company had appointed Captain John Smith the military leader of the colony. There would be no execution.

On May 14, 1607, the voyagers began scratching out a settlement they christened Jamestown. It was not very promising, to say the least. Most of the newcomers fancied themselves gentlemen of leisure and had little taste and less aptitude for the hard work required to claim even a rudimentary living from the wilderness. Food and water were in chronically short supply, and the local Indians—members of Algonquian tribes loosely confederated under a formidable chief, or sachem, the Indians called Wahunsonacock and the colonists came to know as "Powhatan"—were none too friendly. As winter closed in, the colony looked to be on the ragged edge of extinction. Then, in December 1607, Smith went out foraging for food along the Chickahominy River. There, he was suddenly ambushed and taken captive by a group of Powhatan's Indian deer hunters, who carried him to Powhatan at Werowocomoco, the seat of the Powhatan Confederacy on the northern bank of the York River, some fifteen miles north of Jamestown.

Enter Pocahontas.

In all of Virginia's earliest literature, there are just two snippets of narrative concerning her meeting with the captive Smith, both pieces written by Smith himself years after the purported encounter. In 1616, when he was back in London, Smith learned that Pocahontas was coming to visit England with her new husband, Virginia tobacco planter John Rolfe, and would be meeting with Queen Anne and her husband James I. Anxious to ensure that the royals were fully aware of the young Indian woman's credentials and her service to the struggling colony, Smith wrote a letter to his "Most admired Queen":

> The love I bear my God, my King and country, hath so oft emboldened me in the worst of extreme dangers, that now honesty doth constrain me to presume thus far beyond myself, to present your Majesty this short discourse: if

ingratitude be a deadly poison to all honest virtues, I must be guilty of that crime if I should omit any means to be thankful.

So it is, that some ten years ago being in Virginia, and taken prisoner by the power of Powhatan their chief King, I received from this great Salvage [savage] exceeding great courtesy, especially from his son Nantaquaus, the most manliest, comeliest, boldest spirit, I ever saw in a Salvage, and his sister Pocahontas, the Kings most dear and well-beloved daughter, being but a child of twelve or thirteen years of age, whose compassionate pitiful heart, of my desperate estate, gave me much cause to respect her: I being the first Christian this proud King and his grim attendants ever saw: and thus enthralled in their barbarous power, I cannot say I felt the least occasion of want that was in the power of those my mortal foes to prevent, notwithstanding all their threats. After some six weeks fatting amongst those Salvage courtiers, at the minute of my execution, she hazarded the beating out of her own brains to save mine; and not only that, but so prevailed with her father, that I was safely conducted to Jamestown . . .

Eight years after writing this letter, Smith returned to the subject of Pocahontas in his celebrated *Generall Historie of Virginia, New-England, and the Summer Isles* (1624). Writing in the third person (as was his style), Smith elaborated on the encounter:

At last they brought him to Meronocomoco [Werowocomoco], where was Powhatan their Emperor. Here more then [than] two hundred of those grim Courtiers stood wondering at him, as he had beene a monster; till Powhatan and his trayne had put themselues in their greatest braveries. Before a fire vpon a seat like a bedsted, he sat covered with a great robe, made of Rarowcun [raccoon] skinnes, and all the tayles hanging by. On either hand did sit a young wench of 16 to 18 yeares, and along on each side the house, two rowes of men, and behind them as many women, with all their heads and shoulders painted red; many of their heads bedecked with the white downe of Birds; but every one with something: and a great chayne of white beads about their necks. At his entrance before the King, all the people gaue a great shout. The Queene of Appamatuck was appointed to bring him water to wash his hands, and another brought him a bunch of feathers, in stead of a Towell to dry them: having feasted him after their best barbarous manner they could, a long consultation was held, but the conclusion was, two great stones were brought before Powhatan: then as many as could layd hands on him, dragged him to them, and thereon laid his head, and being ready with their clubs, to beate out his braines, Pocahontas the Kings dearest daughter, when no intreaty could prevaile, got his head in her armes, and laid her owne vpon his to saue

him from death: whereat the Emperour was
contented he should liue to make him hatchets,
and her bells, beads, and copper; for they thought
him as well of all occupations as themselues.

On these two brief narratives—but especially that of
1624—the whole Pocahontas romantic mythology is based.
Elaborate mythology and even religious belief flowing
from meager historical sources is not unique to the case of
Pocahontas, of course. The story of Abraham, patriarch of
the Jews and prophet revered by Muslims, Jews, and
Christians alike, occupies at most eighteen pages in
modern printings of the Torah. And in the New Testament
(King James Version), the complete spoken output of Jesus
amounts to a total of just 24,674 words.

As with the biblical sources of religious belief, there is
no shortage of skeptics who question the historical
veracity of the events Smith narrated concerning
Pocahontas. Although, for the most part, the 1616 and
1624 accounts are consistent with each other, Smith iden-
tifies Pocahontas as "a child of twelve or thirteen years of
age" in his letter to Queen Anne, whereas in his *Generall
Historie* he writes of a "young wench of 16 to 18 yeares"
seated on either side of the king. Is one of these supposed
to be Pocahontas? And if so, does this inconsistency
suggest that the entire episode—known, after all, only
through Smith—is a fiction? Or is it a slip of memory? Or,
when writing to his queen, did it suit Smith to describe
Pocahontas as a brave and innocent little girl, whereas
when writing for profit to the general public, did it suit the
purposes of a mercenary veteran to suggest that she was a

sexy "young wench"? Whatever is behind the possible inconsistency, most historians believe that Pocahontas was born about 1595, making her approximately twelve or thirteen years old in 1607.

Skeptics also point to the fact that Smith did not even mention Pocahontas until 1616 and did not publish an account of her until 1624, even though he had already published two widely circulated Virginia narratives prior to 1616—*A True Relation of Such Occurrences and Accidents of Note as Happened in Virginia* (1608) and *A Map of Virginia* (1612)—and a third titled *A Description of New England* in 1616. In *New England's Trials* (1620, 1622), he missed a fourth opportunity to tell her story before finally including the brief narrative in the *Generall Historie* of 1624. At the very least, these skeptics argue, the long lapse of time between the purported Pocahontas episode and its first telling suggests the possibility of Smith's distorted and inflated memory or even deliberate exaggeration. At worst, the fact that he did not include the narrative in his earlier works implies outright fabrication. Others, however, have pointed out that the books published in 1608, 1612, and even 1616 were not autobiographical in nature, but rather geographical and even ethnographical. This line of reasoning suggests that any personal narrative, including the Pocahontas episode, would simply have been out of place in them, whereas the account fits appropriately into the more autobiographical *Generall Historie*.

The only two reasons to doubt Smith's veracity in the case of Pocahontas are that he did have the reputation of being boastful (though not an outright liar) and that no other witness was present to corroborate his testimony.

That the tale of the rescue is appealing and romantic, however, does not mean it is untrue.

But even if John Smith believed he was telling the truth, he still may have gotten it wrong by misunderstanding the very meaning of what had actually happened to him at the hands of Chief Powhatan and his daughter. Smith tells us that he was ambushed and abducted, but if one carefully rereads the 1624 description of his presentation to the chief, Powhatan and his "grim courtiers" are arrayed in elaborate finery, suited either to a religious occasion or one of the highest state. In his earlier letter to Queen Anne, Smith remarked, "I cannot say I felt the least occasion of want that was in the power of those my mortal foes to prevent"—that is, his supposed enemies waited on him hand and foot. Moreover, in the later narrative he does not imply that he was manhandled in any way, let alone beaten or tortured, but, on the contrary: "The Queene of Appamatuck was appointed to bring him water to wash his hands, and another brought him a bunch of feathers, in stead of a Towell to dry them." Next, Smith was "feasted him after their best barbarous manner they could."

In truth, neither historians, ethnographers, nor anthropologists know much of anything about the political and religious customs of the Algonquian tribes of Virginia in the seventeenth century, but in part based on Smith's own narrative, some recent scholars believe that the captain was not being made a permanent captive, let alone prepared for imminent execution; rather, they believe he was undergoing the process of ritual adoption. It was a common practice among many Indian tribes well into the nineteenth century to adopt rather than kill some captives.

Treated with utmost gentleness and courtesy up to the point that "two great stones were brought before Powhatan" and "as many as could layd hands on him, dragged him to them, and thereon laid his head, and being ready with their clubs, to beate out his braines," Smith may well have been subjected to a ritual that was meant to *symbolize* his death as an outsider and his rebirth as a new member of the tribe. It is quite plausible that Pocahontas's role in this ritual was actually well prescribed and thoroughly choreographed. In many tribes, the captive is "adopted" not by order of the male chief, but by the loving gesture of a woman. To be sure, the action of Pocahontas—getting Smith's "head in her armes" and laying "her owne vpon his to saue him from death"—savors of stylized ritual as much as of genuine rescue.

Of course, we can only make an informed guess. But subsequent developments in relations between Powhatan (and his tribes) and the Jamestown colonists suggest that Pocahontas was involved in more than the rescue of a condemned prisoner. There is a story that, in 1608, Pocahontas was moved to intervene a second time to save Smith and other colonists from death at the hands of her father. The sachem had invited Smith and others to an ostensibly cordial meeting at Werowocomoco, but secretly planned to kill them all as they slept. Hearing of this design, Pocahontas supposedly warned her English friends, who posted a guard all night and thereby preempted the massacre.

This story may be true, but it is more likely a fabrication, the product of a later, intensely hostile stage of relations between the Powhatan tribes and the colonists.

While relations between the Indians and the colonists were by no means uniformly peaceful—there were, in fact, frequent skirmishes—the Powhatans could have chosen simply to annihilate Jamestown during the especially harsh winters of 1607, 1608, and 1609. Instead, they aided the colonists during these "starving times," teaching the settlers the rudiments of planting and cultivating the local crops in the local soil. Injured by the explosion of a gunpowder keg in 1609, Smith returned to England. Relations between the colonists and the Indians deteriorated, trade decreased, and the skirmishing intensified, but the two peoples nevertheless continued to coexist.

In his letter to Queen Anne, Captain Smith explicitly attributed such mercy as Powhatan showed the colony to the intercession of Pocahontas. Released from his presumed "captivity" in January 1608, Smith was "safely conducted to Jamestown, . . . where I found about eight and thirty miserable poor and sick creatures, to keep possession of all those large territories of Virginia; such was the weakness of this poor commonwealth, as had the salvages not fed us, we directly had starved. And this relief, most gracious Queen, was commonly brought us by this Lady Pocahontas."

As Smith portrayed it to Queen Anne, Pocahontas was ever the peacemaker: "[W]hen inconstant fortune turned our peace to war, this tender virgin would still not spare to dare to visit us, and by her our jars have been oft appeased, and our wants still supplied." What he wrote next is crucial to understanding what was most likely the true role of Pocahontas in shaping relations between the English colonists and the Native Americans who surrounded them: "were it the policy of her father thus to employ her, or the ordinance of God thus to make her his instrument, or her extraordinary affection to our nation, I know not." For the first time, Smith suggests the possibility that Pocahontas was purposely employed by her father as an ambassador, charged with cementing friendly relations between his tribes and the English.

But why would so powerful a sachem need to use his young daughter in this way? Europeans and, later, Euro-Americans rarely understood the role of a chief or sachem. Typically, they assumed the chief, sachem, or headman was like a king or other European sovereign. The truth is that a Native American chief did not so much rule as merely exercise a certain, often profound degree of influence over his people. In the case of Powhatan, his influence was far-reaching, but it was also spread thin. The thirty-two tribes and two hundred or so villages associated with him were at most a loose confederation over which he exercised nothing approaching absolute or sovereign authority. If he wanted to create friendly relations with the English, the most effective way would have been to encourage the colonists to behave in a friendly manner toward all those tribes associated with him. This would prompt the tribes, in turn, to respond in like manner to the English. Certainly, he could not simply order the thirty-two tribes to act in a certain way. As he may well have seen it, his charming, innocent, and beguiling young daughter—who was also clearly self-assured, courageous, and resourceful—was the perfect instrument to elicit the kind of behavior he desired from the English.

But why would he want to cultivate friendly relations with these weak and vulnerable interlopers, who, if they grew more numerous and more strong, would surely pose a threat to him and his people? Almost certainly, the answer was economic. Powhatan saw in the colonists valuable trading partners whose connections reached far beyond the meager bounds of struggling Jamestown to vast and wealthy empires across the sea. It is a stereotypical error to imagine Indian tribes as insular and isolated, habitually shunning outsiders. Many tribes, including those influenced by Powhatan, lived in part by trade and competed vigorously with one another for it.

In an alliance with the Powhatan Confederacy, Captain John Smith saw the immediate survival of Jamestown. In an alliance with the Jamestown colonists, Powhatan saw economic prosperity. Both Smith and Powhatan saw in Pocahontas the instrument by which an alliance could be forged and, amid fluctuations—for as Smith could not control the behavior of all the colonists, so Powhatan could not simply legislate the policy of thirty-two tribes and two hundred villages—her continued intercession could do much to maintain the peaceful stability conducive to profitable trade.

The assignment Powhatan gave his young daughter would have been an extraordinarily difficult mission even for the most sophisticated of diplomats. While the English and the Indians carried on a lively and mutually profitable trade with one another, they did so in a context of perpetual, mutual distrust rather than easy friendship. After the injured Smith returned to England, with relations between the Powhatans and colonists alternating between small-scale warfare and continued trade, Pocahontas tirelessly shuttled back and forth as her father's emissary.

She had been born Matoaka, a name signifying "little snow feather," but her father had bestowed on her the pet name Pocahontas, meaning (according to some sources) "little wanton" and (according to others) "my favorite daughter." That she was absolutely dutiful toward Powhatan is obvious, yet it is also apparent that she had genuine curiosity about and affection for the English and showed great initiative. She learned their language and served both her father and the colonists well. She must have been a thoroughly remarkable young woman.

In 1613, at a low point in relations between the colony and the Indians, mariner and colonist Samuel Argall tricked Pocahontas into boarding his ship, seized her, and then delivered her to Governor Sir Thomas Dale, who decided to hold her hostage as a means of extorting what he deemed good behavior from the Powhatans or possibly intending to ransom her for the release of English prisoners and the return of stolen weapons and tools. If Pocahontas feared or resented her new coerced status, she never showed it. Instead, she continued to function and behave as if she were a voluntary ambassador rather than a prisoner. She perfected her command of English and thoroughly ingratiated herself with the colonists. By and by, she converted to Christianity and, responding to the overtures of handsome John Rolfe, one of the most prominent and prosperous of the new class of Jamestown tobacco planters, she married him in April 1613 or 1614 (sources differ). She did so, moreover, with the express permission of her father, and in this way made the transition from ambassador to something approaching royalty, as the marriage was intended to restore peace between the tribes and the colony in much the same way that European royal houses intermarried to end wars, solemnize alliances, and seal treaties. The year after the marriage, Powhatan concluded a formal truce with Jamestown, and despite pressures created by the tobacco growers' continued territorial expansion, the uneasy peace endured until Powhatan's death in 1618.

As for Pocahontas, she sailed with her husband, along with Governor Dale and some other Indians, for England in 1616, where James I and Queen Anne greeted her just as John Smith had hoped they would: as a royal princess, the daughter of a king. Her portrait was painted by a court artist, and it portrayed her as every inch the proper Jacobian lady, arrayed in rich European garb save for a Native American feathered fan held in her right hand. The painting that survives is inscribed "Ætatis suæ 21. A^O. 1616" (age 21, 1616).

Pocahontas and Rolfe spent the year in England, planning to return to America in the spring. However, in March 1617, Pocahontas succumbed to illness, possible smallpox, tuberculosis, or pneumonia, in Gravesend. Having been baptized, she was accorded burial in the yard of St. George's Parish Church. Her widowed husband returned to Jamestown alone and died in 1622, possibly as a casualty of a Powhatan uprising under Chief Opechancanough.

∽✆∾

THE COUPLE LEFT BEHIND A SON, Thomas Rolfe, who stayed in England until either 1635 or 1641—sources vary—finally returning to Virginia, where he prospered as a businessman. This is highly significant: *Thomas Rolfe had a colony to return to.* The brief life and remarkable career of Pocahontas had made the survival of Jamestown possible. By the time her father died in 1618 and her uncle waged a fierce half-century war against what were now her people, the colony was too big and too powerful to be wiped out. Opechancanough, nearly one hundred years old and blind, died in 1644, and, in 1646, his successor, Necotowance, granted the colonists legal right to the lands they presently occupied. Jamestown thereby earned the title of the first truly *permanent* English settlement in North America—the seed of a new nation and a new civilization.

TAKEAWAY

PUNCTUATED AS IT WAS BY HOSTILITY and even outright violence, the uneasy alliance between the Jamestown colonists and the Powhatan Indians is a classic instance of a weaker party (the struggling English) forming an alliance with a stronger party (the well-established Powhatan tribes). By any measure, the weaker ally derived the greater benefit from the alliance—namely, survival; however, Chief Powhatan and his people also benefited. He saw an opportunity to establish profitable trade with a new neighbor, and trade was always seen by Indian leaders as a means to power, prestige, and wealth for their people and themselves. In order to make the connection between his tribes and the English without compromising the august appearance of his authority, Powhatan used his daughter, Pocahontas, as an emissary and ambassador.

CHAPTER 3

Gilbert and Sullivan

A Fragile Formula

Previous page: *Poster for* The Mikado, *1885*.

Gilbert and Sullivan

IMAGE ASSEMBLING ONE HUNDRED PEOPLE in one room and another hundred in another room. Entering the first room, you ask for a show of hands: "How many here have heard of Arthur Sullivan?" And then, "How many know the name William Gilbert?" You count hands, then enter the second room. "Please raise your hand," you say to the hundred people assembled there, "if you have heard of Gilbert and Sullivan." Without venturing a guess as to the actual number of raised hands in each of these imaginary rooms, it requires no great powers of speculation to imagine that the raised hands in the second room greatly exceed those raised in the first. The "corporate" name "Gilbert and Sullivan" is far more familiar than the individual names of William Schwenck Gilbert and Arthur Seymour Sullivan. Commercially, aesthetically, culturally, and historically, the phrase "Gilbert and Sullivan" substantially exceeds the sum of its constituent parts.

It was, after all, one of the iconic partnerships, not only in the history of English musical theater, but in all of popular culture. Together, Gilbert and Sullivan wrote fourteen comic operas between 1871 and 1896, including three of the most frequently performed musical stage works ever composed, *H.M.S. Pinafore*, *The Pirates of Penzance*, and *The Mikado*. It is, in fact, widely believed that since 1885, when *The Mikado* premiered at London's Savoy Theatre, not a week has gone by in which that comic opera has *not* been performed by some group—amateur or professional—somewhere in the world. Historically speaking, no musical-theatrical collaboration has produced more commercially successful, more popular, more influential, and more beloved works than Gilbert and Sullivan.

Although it is virtually impossible to think of one without the other, the two men had highly successful careers before 1869, when the composer Frederic Clay, with whom Gilbert was collaborating on a now-forgotten comic opera called *Ages Ago,* introduced his friend Sullivan to Gilbert. The son of a retired Royal Navy surgeon, William Schwenck Gilbert was born in London on November 18, 1836. His father, also named William, was in some ways the typical early Victorian gentleman in that he was a "man of parts," who, in addition to pursuing his vocation as surgeon, occupied his free time by writing reasonably successful novels and short stories, some of which he turned over to his son—an aspiring artist—to illustrate. Young Gilbert followed in his father's footsteps, not in a medical career, but, beginning in 1861, as a writer of stories, humorous articles, theatrical reviews (often in the form of hilarious parodies of the work under review), and light verse, much of the material illustrated by his own artwork. The best of this work was later collected in book form as *Bab Ballads*, "Bab" being his childhood nickname and his first and only *nom de plume.*

In staid Victorian England, the writing of humor was not thought of as a genuine career, and Gilbert tried his hand at civil service employment, which he stood for four years, cordially hating every day of it. Then he tried the military and, briefly, law. He failed miserably as a barrister, however, unable to scare up more than five clients in any given year. Soon, the income from his writing far outweighed what he could bring in by any more "legitimate" means, and in 1863 he wrote his first play, *Uncle Baby*, which enjoyed a seven-week London stage run. Many others followed, including collaborations with composers of light opera. It did not take long for Gilbert to attract a devoted popular following, an audience that recognized and delighted in three shimmering qualities he brought to the stage. First was his deft and fluid command of language, which he wielded with a wit at once polished, sophisticated, hilarious, and disarmingly colloquial. Second, his audiences were charmed, amused, and sometimes even shocked by what critics would universally call his "topsy-turvy" point of view. The British filmmaker Mike Leigh, who in 1999 wrote and directed *Topsy-Turvy*, a film about the creation of *The Mikado*, described Gilbert's unique ability to challenge "our natural expectations" by turning "the world on its head," fusing "opposites with an imperceptible sleight of hand to blend the surreal with the real, and the caricature with the natural . . . to tell a perfectly outrageous story in a completely deadpan way."

The third quality W. S. Gilbert brought to the British stage was salvation. Almost single-handedly, he initiated the reform and rescue of Victorian-age theater. At the time when Gilbert began writing plays, opera libretti, and other theatrical entertainments, English theater was at a dismally low point, both aesthetically and in terms of public repute. A comic genius, Gilbert approached the stage with a new seriousness, developing a rigorous and innovative approach to theatrical production as well as direction, carefully blocking out the actors' movements and gestures, working with them to ensure that his vision was realized perfectly, and insisting on the sanctity of the words he put on the page. Not only did he revolutionize the process and standards by which plays were presented, he made the work of the modern playwright respectable by publishing his plays in book form—something virtually unprecedented for contemporary stage writers.

By the time Clay introduced him to Sullivan, therefore, Gilbert had thoroughly established himself as a commercially and aesthetically successful playwright. For his part, Arthur Seymour Sullivan was also a success. A younger man than Gilbert, he had been born in London on May 13, 1842, the son of a theater musician turned army bandmaster. By the age of eight, young Arthur was playing every instrument in the band, and at twelve he became a child chorister of the Chapel Royal, which often featured him as a soloist. In 1855, one year after becoming a chorister, he wrote—and published!—his first song, "O Israel," and in 1856 he was awarded the coveted Mendelssohn Scholarship, which sent him for study at the Royal Academy of Music. After two years there, Sullivan enrolled in the world's most prestigious music school, the Leipzig Conservatory. He studied at the conservatory from 1858 to 1861, returning to London as a church organist and carrying under his arm the score of his Leipzig graduation-exam piece, a full set of "incidental music" (illustrative musical accompaniment) to Shakespeare's *The Tempest*. The piece was performed at a concert in London's celebrated Crystal Palace in April 1862, making the youthful composer an overnight sensation.

Sullivan was now offered a host of musical jobs, which he avidly accepted. He continued playing the organ, he took on wealthy pupils, he accepted appointment as the first principal of the new National Training School for Music (later the Royal College of Music), he edited music collections and editions for various publishers, and he composed prolifically, turning out religious and secular songs, a highly successful ballet (*L'ile Enchantée*, 1864), and a major choral work (*Kenilworth*, 1864). By 1866, he was receiving numerous commissions, and in that year he also wrote the music for his first comic opera, a popular farce titled *Box and Cox*, followed in 1867 by a two-act operetta, *The Contrabandista*. In 1869, when he first met Gilbert, Sullivan was basking in the triumphant reception of his just-premiered large-scale oratorio, *The Prodigal Son*.

Nothing immediately came of the 1869 meeting of Gilbert and Sullivan, but in 1871 the theatrical producer John Hollingshead commissioned the two men to create a special Christmas entertainment for his Gaiety Theatre. The result, *Thespis*, was a prime early example of Gilbertian topsy-turvyism, in which the Greek gods, having grown too old to do much of anything, are replaced by a troupe of modern actors and actresses in a work that blends a parody of the popular French light opera composer Jacques Offenbach with surprisingly trenchant political satire. Intended only to while away the Christmas season and written in great haste, *Thespis* nevertheless found an unexpectedly enthusiastic audience, who relished both the words and the music and kept the breezy production running for sixty-three sold-out performances.

Despite the success of *Thespis*, Gilbert and Sullivan returned to their separate careers, Gilbert turning out a number of new stage works and Sullivan composing another grand oratorio, a major song cycle, incidental music to Shakespeare's *Merry Wives of Windsor*, and a succession of songs and hymns, the most enduring of which was "Onward, Christian Soldiers." Then, it seems, fate took a hand.

In 1874, composer-producer Carl Rosa commissioned Gilbert to write a libretto for a short opera to be called *Trial by Jury*, in which Rosa's wife was to sing the lead. Her sudden death in childbirth, however, put a tragic end to the project and left Gilbert with a libretto for which no music—or stage—existed. In another corner of the small world of London theater, Richard D'Oyly Carte, manager of the Royalty Theatre, had heard about the libretto, and it so happened that he was just then in desperate need of a short piece to fill out an evening during which the main attraction was Jacques Offenbach's popular but brief *La Périchole*. Carte called on Gilbert and suggested that Arthur Sullivan be brought in to furnish a score. For his part, Sullivan found the libretto delightful, and within a few weeks he had completed the score of *Trial by Jury*.

The short opera foreshadowed what would be the essence of a typical Gilbert and Sullivan piece.

On the face of it, *Trial by Jury* was nothing more than a satirical spoof of law and lawyers, but its exuberant silliness was thoughtfully anchored by Gilbert's training and experience as a barrister. It had real substance. The libretto took itself seriously—and that's precisely what made it so funny. At issue was a suit for breach of promise of marriage. The defendant's absurd defense was that he should get off lightly because he was such a dreadfully bad man that the plaintiff was actually fortunate that he had decided not to marry her. The plaintiff's equally absurd counter to this was that she loved the defendant so deeply that she should be awarded "substantial damages" at his expense. In the end, the judge turned this topsy-turvy situation on its head and settled the matter by marrying the plaintiff himself. Sullivan grasped the aesthetics of the premise and its realization brilliantly, providing a comically serious score that perfectly showcased the deadpan absurdity of the libretto. The result was a hit. Intended to fill out a short theatrical bill, *Trial by Jury* instead took on a life of its own. The show was not only featured at the Royalty but also taken on tour subsequently. It is still performed today.

Carte and other London impresarios now pressed Gilbert and Sullivan for more, but the parties proved unable to reach a mutually satisfactory arrangement. The librettist and composer did respond favorably, however, to Carte's suggestion that he mount a revival of their earlier collaboration, *Thespis*, but then Carte found himself unable to raise the money for the production.

Disappointed but undaunted, Carte refused to give up. He was, after all and in his own right, as remarkable a figure as either Gilbert or Sullivan. Whereas Gilbert had sought to rehabilitate the London stage, Carte wanted to foster a uniquely English brand of light opera to replace the French imports, mostly Offenbach's works, which monopolized his own Royalty as well as other London theaters. He was a capable minor composer himself, having written songs, instrumental works, and even four comic operas, but he realized that his true talent was as a producer and manager, a theatrical man of business. Determined now to midwife and then manage a partnership between Gilbert and Sullivan, he found backers and put together a syndicate to finance what he dubbed the Comedy Opera Company. In 1877, he leased a small theater called the Opera Comique and, armed with his investors' cash, successfully commissioned a new work from the librettist and composer. Titled *The Sorcerer*, it was a smash hit, and it was followed the very next year by *H.M.S. Pinafore*. Carte anticipated that the new work, a seagoing satire on the rise of good-natured incompetents to positions of great power, would create a sensation. Both Gilbert and Sullivan threw themselves into the production, each of the players approaching their roles with comically devastating earnestness. Gilbert created a libretto full of realistic details and rich in characterization, while Sullivan produced a brilliant score and prepared the musicians personally and to perfection.

Despite all their work, initial response to *Pinafore* was lukewarm, and the investors in the Comedy Opera Company voted to close the show and cut their losses. With his own confidence unshaken, Carte proposed to Gilbert and Sullivan that they join him in forming a new company. The three thus organized the D'Oyly Carte Opera Company, which would be dedicated exclusively to producing the works of Gilbert and Sullivan. Although history chiefly remembers the partnership of the librettist and composer, the producer—the impresario-manager—played a catalytic role in this commercial and aesthetic alliance. The D'Oyly Carte Opera Company remained in operation until 1982, long after the deaths of all the principals.

As presented by the D'Oyly Carte Company, *H.M.S. Pinafore* went on to achieve unprecedented success, and

Gilbert, who had found in Sullivan a composer entirely compatible with his own aesthetic, went on to extend this sense of creative reliability to the actors themselves. Traditionally, playwrights and theatrical producers hired established stars to bring their works successfully to life. With Carte's approval, Gilbert stood this tradition on its head. He decided to use his plays to create his own stars. Everything about each production would, in effect, be a known quantity. He had a congenial composer. He would supervise set design, costuming, and all aspects of stage direction. He would enforce absolute fidelity to his scripts. And he would create an ongoing ensemble, which would be dedicated exclusively to the performance of Gilbert and Sullivan. It was the founding of what became a standard method of theatrical production: the repertory system.

And for a long time, play after play, it all worked remarkably well. After *H.M.S. Pinafore* came *The Pirates of Penzance* in 1879, followed by *Patience* in 1881. During the run of this play, Carte built a new theater, the Savoy, expressly to showcase Gilbert and Sullivan. Much larger and more modern than the Opera Comique, it was the first theater in the world to be exclusively lit by electric lighting. *Patience* continued its run at the new Savoy and was followed by *Iolanthe* in 1882 and *Princess Ida* in 1884.

Although *Princess Ida* was by no means a failure, it did prove significantly less successful than its predecessors, and this aggravated what was becoming an increasingly stressful alliance between Gilbert and Sullivan. Back during the run of *Trial by Jury* in 1875, the reviewer for the *Times* of London had written, "It seems, as in the great Wagnerian operas, as though poem and music had proceeded simultaneously from one and the same brain." Years later, the great British conductor Sir Henry Wood elaborated on this perception, commenting that Sullivan's "music is perfectly appropriate to the words of which it is the setting." Sullivan, Wood wrote, "found the right, the only cadences to fit Gilbert's happy and original rhythms." Gilbert himself had once explained that although he was not at all musical, the process by which he wrote lyrics always began with finding the right rhythm. Only after that was set did the words follow. Wood continued: not only did Sullivan possess an uncanny ability to create music that fit Gilbert's rhythms, the music also matched "Gilbert's fun," throwing "Gilbert's frequent irony, pointed although not savage, into relief." Lest he give the impression that Sullivan was simply and entirely subject to Gilbert, however, Wood observed that his "music is much more than the accompaniment to Gilbert's libretti, just as Gilbert's libretti are far more than words to Sullivan's music. We have two masters who are playing a concerto. Neither is subordinate to the other; each gives what is original, but the two, while neither predominates, are in perfect correspondence. This rare harmony of words and music is what makes these operas entirely unique. They are the work not of a musician and his librettist nor of a poet and one who sets his words to music, but of two geniuses." What the *Times* reviewer hinted at and what Sir Henry Wood elaborated upon was the very essence of a successful alliance: the partnership of equals, each of whom brings to the association something the other does not possess but is capable of fully using. The result is synergy, a whole far greater than the sum of its parts.

Unfortunately, by 1883, Arthur Sullivan was no longer seeing it this way. He surely enjoyed the monetary rewards of his collaboration with Gilbert, but he was feeling increasing pressure from friends, musical colleagues, and critics to create something more "serious," more "lofty" than mere tunes to showcase Gilbert's words. Worse, he himself was keenly aware of having to subordinate his process to that of Gilbert. He felt that he had to, in effect, dumb down his scores so as not to obscure Gilbert's words. In true grand opera, the librettist took a backseat to the composer. Indeed, the precedence of the composer was reflected in the traditional manner in which composer and lyricist were credited in songs or operas. The composer's name always came first, the lyricist/librettist's second. Not so, however, in the case of *Gilbert* and Sullivan.

The disappointing reception of *Princess Ida* moved Sullivan to complain to Carte that "it is impossible for me to do another piece of the character of those already written by Gilbert and myself." To Gilbert, he said that he had "come to the end of my tether" and moaned about his fatigue at composing songs that were nothing more than "syllable-setting," the music "never allowed to rise and speak for itself."

Although Sullivan now wanted to terminate the alliance with Gilbert, he was not free to do so. He had just signed a five-year contract with Carte to produce a new opera with Gilbert on six months' notice. And Carte responded to Sullivan's complaints by invoking the contract and calling for a new opera.

In an agony of frustration, fearing that his reputation, his further artistic development, and his creative freedom were in grave jeopardy, Sullivan appealed to Gilbert at the very least to endeavor to produce something different. Sullivan's principal complaint about Gilbert's stories was that their plots were becoming repetitive, formulaic—even mechanical—all too often turning on some arbitrary and improbable artificial contrivance such as the working of a magic potion, "lozenge," or elixir. His music, he pleaded with Gilbert, cried out for a story with genuine probability and real *human* emotion.

Now it was Gilbert's turn to despair. His genius, he felt, was founded on his sense of the topsy-turvy, which by its very nature relied on a certain arbitrary, magical, even mechanical quality of contrivance. How, then, could he reconcile this with what Sullivan now demanded? The partnership, indeed, appeared to be doomed—until Gilbert had an inspiration, an inspiration filled with genuine probability and human emotion, an inspiration without potion, lozenge, or elixir.

Writing in *The New-York Daily Tribune* on August 9, 1885, Gilbert told the story of this inspiration and its product. "In May, 1884," he explained, "it became necessary to decide upon a subject for the next Savoy opera." Given the combined pressures of the Carte contract and Arthur Sullivan's discontent, this sentence, we know, was a profound understatement. "A Japanese executioner's sword hanging on the wall of my library . . . suggested the broad idea upon which the libretto is based." From this sword, *The Mikado* was born. Its central character would be the very embodiment of the Gilbertian topsy-turvy aesthetic, yet the essence of this particular instance of topsy-turvydom would be utterly human rather than arbitrarily magical. The executioner's sword suggested the character of an executioner. Seen through the inverted lens of Gilbert's creative genius, however, the executioner was "an exceptionally tender-hearted person whose natural instincts were in direct opposition to his official duties." This character settled upon, Gilbert invented the rest of the cast, each topsy-turvily suited to a specific member of the Savoy repertory company.

Thus, Gilbert continued in his *Tribune* piece, the creative process began with a sword, then proceeded through characters and casting. "The next thing was to decide upon two scenes which should be characteristic and effective." From these scenes, "the story of the piece had to be drawn up in narrative form," and the "story . . . next divided into two acts, and the sequence of events in each act . . . decided upon, with the exits and entrances sketched out, the purport of the various dialogues suggested, and the musical situations arranged." This, Gilbert explained, was the "'*scenario*' (that is the technical name for the piece in its skeleton form)."

At this "skeleton" stage, "I read the story and scenario to Sir Arthur Sullivan. He approved of the story, made some valuable suggestions bearing chiefly on the musical situations, and after three or four hours of careful deliberation the chain of events was finally determined, and a twelfth and last version of the story . . . was prepared the next day." Only then was the libretto actually begun. In "its first form," Gilbert wrote, the libretto "is simply the scenario reduced to dialogue of the baldest and simplest nature, leaving the songs to be written afterward." Once he had sketched out the dialogue, he put the libretto aside and turned "to the words of the songs."

My normal practice is to furnish Sir Arthur Sullivan with the songs of the first act, and while he is setting them I proceed with the songs of Act Two. When these are practically finished I revert to the dialogue, elaborating and polishing the crude suggestions contained in the first version of the libretto, while he composes the music, and so it comes to pass that the pianoforte [non-orchestrated] score and the libretto are usually completed at about the same date.

The next step was reading the libretto to the company that would perform it. However, "as the piece is an opera, the company must learn the music before they begin to study the dialogue and action." Sullivan and his "next in command, Mr. Frank Cellier" proceeded to conduct two weeks of music rehearsals, which Gilbert made it a practice to attend, partly to get "the rhythm of the musical numbers . . . , partly [to arrange] details of scenery with the scenic artist, partly [to arrange] details of costume, but chiefly [to determine] the 'stage management' of the piece": the movement and blocking of the actors, which Gilbert planned out by manipulating small blocks of wood on a scale-model stage.

After the musical rehearsals were completed and the scenic, costume, and blocking decisions made, four weeks were devoted to stage rehearsals. "As soon as the details of the first act are roughly settled, Sir Arthur Sullivan usually attends a [stage] rehearsal in order to see that the proposed 'business' [actions, movements] is not inconsistent with his musical effects, and this visit usually results in a certain amount of rearrangement." With self-deprecating modesty, Gilbert continued: "He is the most self-sacrificing and unselfish of composers, but even his good-nature is not proof against an arrangement whereby the chorus dance a wild jig during an elaborate *cadenza* or an unaccompanied quartet. But when a composer works with a librettist who is deaf, dumb and blind on all musical points, he is not unprepared for professional solecisms of this description."

There can be no doubt that the partnership of Gilbert and Sullivan was a collaboration in the fullest sense, yet despite Gilbert's generosity in his *Tribune* article, it is clear from this description that Sullivan was right. He was indeed obliged to follow Gilbert's lead. Gilbert supplied the original idea for a work, Gilbert wrote the story, and Gilbert wrote the lyrics. Only then did Sullivan go to work. During rehearsals there was clearly a greater degree of genuine give and take, but otherwise, Gilbert was the dominant member of the alliance.

Premiering in 1885, *The Mikado* is generally considered Gilbert and Sullivan's masterpiece, and it is beautifully evident that the humanity of the story drew out the very best in Sullivan's music. There is unquestionably an incandescent charm to the work, which remains as popular as it ever was. *The Mikado* was followed by *Ruddigore* in 1887, *Yeoman of the Guard* in 1888, and *The Gondoliers* in 1889. *Ruddigore* was only moderately successful, and although *Yeoman* and *The Gondoliers* fared better, Sullivan nevertheless complained bitterly: "I am a cipher in the theatre."

By 1890, Sir Arthur Sullivan could stand it no more. At last yielding to pressure from the "serious" musical

community—and to his own hunger for artistic freedom—
he decided to begin writing a true grand opera, in which he,
the composer, would take precedence. It was to be *Ivanhoe*,
based on the novel by Sir Walter Scott. It is a measure of
Sullivan's high regard for his long-time collaborator that
he asked Gilbert to write the libretto, but Gilbert instantly
declined, pointing out that "the librettist of grand opera is
always swamped by the composer," and that was a reversal
of roles he was not prepared to accept.

In the meantime, however, Carte had proposed to
finance and build the Royal English Opera House in
London near Covent Garden to showcase English operas,
beginning with *Ivanhoe*. At this very time, on April 22,
1890, Gilbert wrote to Sullivan concerning "a difficulty" he
was having with Carte. "I was appalled to learn from him
that the preliminary expenses of the *Gondoliers* amounted
to the stupendous sum of £4,500!!!" Gilbert asked to
examine the ledgers and discovered "the most surprising
item . . . £500 for new carpets *for the front of the house*!" This
Gilbert took to be a violation of the 1883 contract with the
Savoy, which deducted from the revenues generated by the
Gilbert and Sullivan operas only the "expenses and charges
of producing" them and any "repairs incidental to the
performance." New carpeting, Gilbert protested, could not
be honestly classified as "repairs incidental to the performance." This incident quickly escalated into what Gilbert
and Sullivan scholars call the "Carpet Quarrel" between
Carte and Gilbert, but the real crisis came when Gilbert
called on Sullivan for support, and Sullivan—doubtless
thinking of *Ivanhoe* and the new opera house—sided with
Carte. On May 5, 1890, Gilbert sent Sullivan a letter: "The

time for putting an end to our collaboration has at last arrived." A lawsuit against Carte also followed, resulting in a partial judgment in Gilbert's favor. Carte paid him £1,000 in addition to the £2,000 in *Gondolier* proceeds that had already been rendered to him.

❧

THE "CARPET QUARREL" WAS THE PROVERBIAL LAST straw in what had been an extraordinary but inherently fragile alliance, involving as it did the egos of two fiercely creative men. Yet the camel's back was not quite broken. In 1893, Gilbert and Sullivan collaborated on *Utopia, Limited* and, in 1896, on *The Grand Duke*, both for D'Oyly Carte, but neither was very successful. Four years after this last opera, Sir Arthur Sullivan, chronically in frail health, succumbed to heart failure during a bout of pneumonia. He died on November 22, 1900, at the age of fifty-eight. Gilbert would create four more stage works before he died in 1911, but none were successful at the time of their production, and none are remembered today. What he wrote in 1904 may not have been precisely accurate in the most literal sense, but it was nevertheless true: "Savoy opera was snuffed out by the deplorable death of my distinguished collaborator, Sir Arthur Sullivan. When that event occurred, I saw no one with whom I felt that I could work with satisfaction and success, so I discontinued to write *libretti*."

TAKEAWAY

IN THEORY, THE PARTNERSHIP OF Gilbert and Sullivan was the perfect alliance. It brought together two men of equal genius, the masters of precisely complementary arts, comic verse and comedic music—the one man, in effect, leaving off precisely where the other began. At the height of their collaboration, Gilbert and Sullivan produced work far greater than either could produce separately or, for that matter, with other partners. Together, their sum was indeed greater than the parts that constituted it. The problem came when theory met real life. An alliance of equals, especially of prodigious equals, is always a delicate matter, subject to the ego, will, whim, or sensitivity of one partner or the other. The moment one partner perceives himself diminished or compromised by the other, the alliance typically begins to crumble, no matter how successful the products it has produced.

CHAPTER 4

The Brothers Wright

A Saga of Maximum Synergy

Previous page: *The Wright Brothers' first flight, Kitty Hawk, North Carolina, December 17, 1903.*

The Brothers Wright

T HEY WERE READY TO FLY, they believed, at about 2:40 on the afternoon of December 14, 1903. The aircraft they had together dreamed up, designed, and built looked more like a box kite than a modern machine. It was mounted on what the brothers dubbed "Grand Junction Railroad," a sixty-foot-long monorail laid down the sandy slope of Big Kill Devil Hill at Kitty Hawk, North Carolina, a testing ground they had chosen, based on data from the U.S. Weather Service, for its mild climate and steady prevailing winds. One of the brothers—no one knows which—thrust a hand in his pocket, retrieved a coin, and flipped it. Wilbur Wright won the toss, and so was tapped to become the first human being to make a controlled, sustained, powered flight in a heavier-than-air craft.

Linger a moment on the coin toss.

The decision to let a momentous issue ride on the toss of a coin is no decision at all, but rather the abrogation of decision. The collaboration of the Wright Brothers was one of history's most iconic partnerships, a brilliant division of labor that enabled two bicycle mechanics, entirely self-taught in the field of aeronautics and working without government or corporate funding of any kind, to do what human beings had been dreaming of for centuries. Yet at the culmination, the arrival of the moment to fly at last, the brothers ceased their rational decision making and instead committed the final issue to random chance. Perhaps this remarkable abandonment of rationality is the most compelling evidence we have of the profound depth of the brothers' collaboration. It was as if neither could decide where one left off and the other began.

Who am I? Who are you? Toss a coin.

Wilbur Wright was born in 1867, Orville in 1871. They did not look much like brothers. Wilbur stood about five-ten, but, angular and bony, he appeared even taller. By 1903 he was prematurely bald, face long and typically unsmiling, his lips thin and tightly set, resembling, according to a French journalist, nothing more strongly than a bird. Standing perhaps an inch and a half shorter than Wilbur, Orville appeared to be much shorter because he was somewhat heavier. In contrast to his bronze-faced brother, his complexion was downright pallid, his fair skin set off by his full head of dark, albeit thinning, hair. (Orville actually worked to achieve his pallor, countering the effects of the sun at Kitty Hawk by liberally applying lemon juice to bleach his skin.) Whereas Wilbur was always clean-shaven, Orville sported a thick red mustache verging on the handlebar style.

Even more striking than the differences in their appearance, were the contrasts in their temperaments. Wilbur was quiet, calm, deliberate, and fearless, whereas Orville was impulsive, nervous, painfully shy, and—some even thought—quite timid. In the process of inventing the airplane, Orville did much of the grunt work, while Wilbur formulated concepts and functioned as the public face of the team. He was a talented, fluent lecturer, whereas Orville was deathly afraid of speaking before an audience and, indeed, never did.

Despite striking differences in appearance and personality, the young men's father, Milton, insisted that they had always been as "inseparable as twins," and in 1903 both still lived beneath what Milton liked to call "the paternal roof." Neither ever married. It is not that the two were identical—quite the opposite was the case—but that precisely where one left off the other began. The strength of one in a particular area compensated for the weakness of the other in that same area. For instance, while historians generally agree that the idea to create an airplane originated with Wilbur, it was Orville's sheer nervous energy that drove the project to successful completion.

They meshed like the gears of a fine machine, and in the end they had the really important things in common: a keen capacity for close observation and analysis, a facile mechanical aptitude, and an ability to translate what they observed and analyzed into concrete, working reality. Most crucial of all, they shared a passion to fly. When what was intended to have been the maiden flight, on December 14, 1903, failed—the aircraft lifting off no more than fifteen feet before stalling and falling back into the sand—the brothers made some repairs and were ready to try again on December 17. This time, there was no talk of coin-tossing. There was no need for it. Both agreed wordlessly that Wilbur had had his chance, so now it was time for Orville to take over. There was no discussion, no need for it. It was simply the way things were. One left off, the other began.

The boys shook hands shortly after 10:30 in the morning. Orville took his position, prone on his belly across the center of the lower wing. The engine coughed into life, the counter-rotating propellers turned, Orville shifted a lever that held the plane motionless on its monorail track, and down the track it moved. It was 10:35

when the aircraft lifted off, and it was still 10:35 when it landed just twelve seconds later, having flown a distance of some 120 feet.

That was it, the first powered human flight. Before the day was over, Wilbur took a turn, flying 195 feet, then Orville again—200 feet over 15 seconds—before Wilbur covered what seemed a marathon distance of 852 feet in 59 seconds.

Both Orville and Wilbur Wright were meticulous note takers. Much of what they did was, by necessity, of a trial-and-error nature, but their careful notes ensured that, laborious though the trials and errors were, they would never be unnecessarily repetitive. One of the few items they did not bother to note was who did what. Family members and friends of the brothers always remarked that Wilbur was naturally the dominant of the two, and it is clear that the Wrights' serious fascination with aeronautics began with Wilbur. Yet by about 1900, when the two were building experimental gliders, they made an unmistakably deliberate effort to disguise the precedence of one brother over the other. The first person singular was banished from virtually all of their correspondence and replaced with "we." Even checks were signed "The Wright Brothers" and were always drawn against their single joint account. When Wilbur lectured about their aeronautical experiments, he credited all ideas and actions jointly, as if the brothers were an entirely corporate "person."

If Wilbur was ever tempted to seize the lion's share of credit for himself, he never betrayed even a hint of such temptation. Was this a sign of altruism or fraternal love? Possibly. There is no doubt that the brothers loved one another deeply. More likely, however, both Orville and

Wilbur recognized that, as a sum, they were far greater than they were as parts. This was not just because they happened to be brothers. No law of nature dictates that brothers necessarily work well together. It is not for nothing that one of the first stories in the Old Testament concerns a fraternal bond that went very bad very quickly. But having grown up together, the Wrights understood each other and had spent a lifetime perfecting their perfect "fit." Orville's personality verged on reclusiveness, but Wilbur was quite outgoing. Nevertheless, together, the brothers had something of an us-against-the-world mentality, which came to the fore shortly after they began producing airplanes commercially and became embroiled in years of bitter, ultimately counterproductive lawsuits over patent issues. At the height of these legal battles, some described the Wrights as "paranoid." Maybe. But theirs was always a paranoia *à deux,* never the delusion of one *or* the other.

Wilbur, with his initial interest in aeronautics, was the spark. He was able to identify the fundamental theoretical issues of flight, essentially deciding that the basics of lift and power had been solved—not optimally, by any means, but the fundamentals had been established. What remained largely unaddressed was the issue of control—"equilibrium," Wilbur called it—and he concluded that "the problem of equilibrium constituted the problem of flight itself."

It was a breakthrough insight in part born of Wilbur Wright's experience with bicycles. At the turn of the nineteenth century, the bicycle was not a child's toy but a sophisticated, cutting-edge mode of personal transport. Anyone with reasonably healthy legs could supply sufficient power to move a bicycle. What took skill and required practice was attaining and maintaining control of the machine: achieving equilibrium. The analogy to flight was, as Wilbur conceived it, unmistakable.

But how was control to be achieved?

In later writings, Wilbur shared with Orville all the credit for answering this question, yet clearly it was Wilbur—and Wilbur alone—who did the initial conceptual thinking. The Wrights' most important predecessor in experimentation with manned flight was the German aeronaut Otto Lilienthal. His approach to control was merely to use his own shifting body weight to change the center of gravity of the gliders he flew. The result? In 1896, Lilienthal was killed when he lost control of his glider and crashed. Wilbur pondered Lilienthal's method of equilibrium in relation to that of the most successful fliers in nature, birds. He concluded that, in contrast to Lilienthal, birds used "more positive and energetic methods of regaining equilibrium than that of shifting the center of gravity." They achieved control not just by shifting their body weight, but by turning the leading edge of one wingtip up and the other down. They *warped* their wings.

It was one thing to warp a wing of nerve, muscle, tendon, bone, and feathers, but quite another to do the same for an artificial wing of nothing more than inert wood and fabric. The solution hit Wilbur quite by accident or, at least, without conscious effort. He was working in his bicycle shop one July day in 1899 when the rectangular box in which an inner tube had been packed caught his eye. The end tabs had been ripped off of the box. Taking the empty, open-ended box in his two hands, he twisted it. And there it was. Make a wing that could be twisted in a controlled fashion.

Everyone who knew the Wright brothers knew that Wilbur was the dominant one, the one who had the ideas, but Orville was always the more mechanically inclined of the two. Both he and Wilbur were mechanics—eminently practical men—but Wilbur, quick to grasp and formulate concepts, was the born theoretician, whereas Orville was the born inventor. More precisely, he was a facile innovator. As a youngster, he built himself a printing press. As a bicycle mechanic, he innovated and improved the design of the existing wheel hub. Later, in 1913, he was awarded the Collier Trophy in aeronautics for his breakthrough invention of a practical automatic pilot, a development far ahead of its time. Much later, toward the end of his life, he innovated an improvement to the flaps on World War II–vintage dive bombers, creating a split-flap design that enhanced control and made it easier to pull out of steep dives. Even at home, he was constantly tinkering, creating innovations to plumbing and heating systems and even crafting a combination bread slicer and toaster, which produced breakfast toast that was browned to perfection.

Once Wilbur, the scientist, had formulated the concept and provided the model for achieving control, Orville, the inventor, pitched in with the building of miniature model wings using bamboo, paper, and strings. After trying these out, the brothers were satisfied that they had a good proof of concept and went on to build an unmanned biplane kite with a five-foot wingspan, the warp of its wings controlled by means of strings attached to sticks held in the kite flier's hand. They flew this successfully in August 1899 and then went on to build what Wilbur called a "man-carrying machine." Together, they experimented with it, soon reaching the conclusion that a man flying in a tethered box kite could never achieve proper control. Even carrying a man, a kite was just a kite. The only alternative was to cut the cord and take the hazardous step of building and piloting an untethered, free-flying manned glider—in effect, a revised version of the infernal machine that had killed Otto Lilienthal.

They returned to Kitty Hawk in 1901 with a glider sporting wings they had shaped to specifications based on calculations made by earlier aeronautical experimenters. The glider flew, but, to the brothers' chagrin, just barely, its wings providing no more than a third of the lift the numbers had predicted. After much tweaking—probably mostly by Orville—they got the craft to fly somewhat better, but still poorly and far below expectation.

It was a deeply dejected Wilbur Wright who, on the train back to Dayton, turned to his brother. "Not within a thousand years would man ever fly!" he said.

If those who knew the brothers were right, it was now up to Orville to rekindle Wilbur's guttering flame. Whereas in the glider experiments Wilbur saw the failure of theory, Orville concentrated on the fact that the glider *had* flown—just not as well as the numbers said it should. Was it Orville or Wilbur who, by the time they reached Dayton, suggested that the mistake they had made was in simply assuming that the problem of lift had been entirely solved by others? Was it Orville or Wilbur who asked, *What if the numbers are wrong?*

We don't know, but Orville—shy and retiring—was nevertheless the more energetic and optimistic of the Wrights. Chances are that it was he who questioned the received wisdom recorded in the existing lift tables. As usual, there is absolutely no way to guess who came up with the next invention, the world's first wind tunnel, which the brothers used to test scores of wing shapes, carefully measuring the lift provided by each in order to arrive at their own lift calculations. It is known that while these experiments were under way, Orville, assisted by engineer Charles Taylor, assumed the principal responsibility for building a lightweight gasoline motor to power the next flight, together with a system of pulleys and cables to "warp" the trailing edges of the wings in opposite directions. As always, where Wilbur had left off, Orville began.

T HE WRIGHT BROTHERS WERE A TWO-MAN *TEAM,* in the fullest sense of the word. Field, say, a baseball team, and you would be foolish to deploy nine players who excelled at precisely the same specialty. You need a diversity of talents, good outfielders and players adept at playing the various base positions, plus an agile shortstop. You need a specialized pitcher, and an equally skilled catcher. Ideally, one member takes up and fills in where another leaves off. This is a lesson typically ignored in the workplace. Asked to put together a team for a given project, what do most leaders do? They put out the call for "creative people" and assemble, say, a group of nine men and women who excel at coming up with good ideas. What could be wrong with this? Well, only this: a team that ends up with nine really good ideas has failed to accomplish its mission. There is more to be done. The best idea must be selected, refined, and implemented. Trouble is that a team consisting only of idea generators is like a baseball team made up of nine really good pitchers. You need more to play the game, just as the project team needs creative types as well as people who are good at criticizing ideas, people who are good at refining ideas, and people who know how to implement them. Take note: a *good* RISK player is entirely self-reliant. A *great* RISK player knows when to team up with others, but only as long as those others can provide a point of view or a skill the "great" player lacks.

TAKEAWAY

A TEAM IS NEVER ABOUT DUPLICATION of effort, but amplification of effort—synergy. If both the Wrights had been theoreticians, they would not have flown—not on December 17, 1903, and probably not "within a thousand years." But their alliance was strategic, the one brother starting the work, the other sustaining it, refining it, and cheering it on. As the more theoretically oriented of the pair, Wilbur doubtless had a passion for the truth, so when he insisted on sharing credit equally with his brother, presenting to the world a solid corporate front, he was not being generous. He was just telling the truth.

CHAPTER 5

The Best of Enemies

The Hitler-Stalin Pact

∾↶↷∾

Previous page: *Vyacheslav Molotov signs the German-Soviet nonaggression pact; Joachim von Ribbentrop and Josef Stalin stand behind him, Moscow, August 23, 1939.*

The Best of Enemies

T O THE PEOPLE OF SPAIN, the bitter Spanish Civil War of 1936–39 was just that—a civil war—but to the Soviet Union on the one hand and Italy and Germany (with the connivance of Portugal) on the other, it was a proxy war to which all three nations committed troops, arms, aircraft, and aid. As much of the rest of the world saw it, the war was neither first or last a civil conflict nor a war between competing national interests, but a winner-take-all contest between diametrically opposed ideologies, communism versus fascism (of which German Nazism was deemed a subset), whose champions contended in the dust of Spain for nothing less than the future of the world. For idealists in the generation that came of age between the twentieth century's two world wars, the Spanish Civil War was a morally and intellectually defining event, not merely a contest between political philosophies, but a struggle of good against evil on a scale worthy of Milton's *Paradise Lost:* a battle royal between God and the devil.

By the period of the Spanish Civil War, the world had been languishing in the depths of the Great Depression for more than half a decade. In this economic climate, both communism and fascism loomed as alternatives to democratic capitalism, which, to many, seemed to have utterly failed, the solutions it proposed to economic and social crisis proving tentative, feeble, and feckless. To many, the war in Spain was a call not just to arms, but to choose between the only two viable ideologies left standing. Liberals, including many in the United States and the other Western democracies, threw their support behind the leftist Spanish

"Loyalists," backed by the Soviets, and in opposition to the fascist insurgents, led chiefly by the Spanish general Francisco Franco and supported by Benito Mussolini and Adolf Hitler. Some plucky and committed young people volunteered to fight for the Loyalists—many Americans joining the Abraham Lincoln Brigade—but even among those who did not choose to go to war, it seemed that the question on every lip was "Which side are you on?" A number of people, including many young intellectuals, believed that there were only two choices, the one good, the other evil.

With so many of the world's leaders steeped, it seemed, in a moral twilight, and with nations mired in an international economy stalled and stagnant, the ideological clarity of left versus right, of communism versus fascism, shone as a beacon, irresistible to the international class of young, politically active intellectuals. For this group especially, the conflict provided a much-needed occasion for self-definition. It made sense of the world.

Then, on August 24, 1939, that sense was suddenly shattered. Early on this morning, Germany's foreign minister, Joachim von Ribbentrop, and his Soviet counterpart, Vyacheslav Molotov, signed the "Treaty of Non-Aggression between Germany and the Union of Soviet Socialist Republics," a document better known as the Molotov-Ribbentrop Pact or the Hitler-Stalin Pact, in which sworn ideological foes made a show of solidarity.

The published portion of the treaty was a nonaggression pact, both sides obligating "themselves to desist from any act of violence, any aggressive action, and any attack on each other, either individually or jointly with other Powers." Germany and the Soviet Union disavowed participation in "any grouping of Powers . . . that is directly or indirectly aimed at the other party," and they agreed to settle any disputes that might arise between one another "exclusively through friendly exchange of opinion or, if necessary, through the establishment of arbitration commissions." On the surface, this disavowal of aggression should have brought a measure of stability to a world verging on war, but most of that world saw it as nothing less than an outright alliance between the two great totalitarian powers, an alliance that would enable either or both to conduct war without fear of interference. Had the world also been privy to the "Secret Additional Protocol" appended to the pact, the shock and dismay would have been even more overwhelming. The protocol provided for a German-Soviet partition of Poland—in effect, a division of that nation between the two signatories—and cleared the way for Soviet occupation of the Baltic states, including Finland, Estonia, Latvia, and Lithuania. In short, the secret protocol made a war of aggression virtually inevitable, with Germany and the Soviet Union operating as allies. It paved the way for the invasion and conquest of Poland and the Baltic countries.

Stunned, the ideological idealists of 1939 felt a betrayal of great magnitude and one they simply could not comprehend. What business could Hitler the Nazi and Stalin the Communist possibly have with one another? Worst of all, it was Stalin who had approached Hitler—through Molotov via Ribbentrop. How could the inheritor of Lenin's mantle, the avatar of Marxist equality and social justice both seek and conclude a pact with the devil, the very leader against whom Stalin himself had fought in Spain, and Stalin's followers throughout Europe had battled in the streets of Europe and even those of Germany itself?

Had the idealists read their Marx more carefully, the Hitler-Stalin Pact would not have seemed to them quite so shocking. Ideologue though he was, Marx also embraced the doctrine of *Realpolitik*, the late-nineteenth-century approach to international relations in which ideals and ideology took a backseat to pragmatic advantage. Stalin allowed himself to be portrayed popularly as an ideologue, absolutely committed to the great hearts-and-minds struggle between communism and fascism, but the conclusion of the Hitler-Stalin Pact revealed him to be what he had, in fact, always been, a practitioner of Realpolitik above all else.

Stalin made a great show of supporting the Loyalists in Spain, fighting there the fascists of Italy and the Nazis of Germany. Yet even while he conducted this campaign, billed as an ideological war, he initiated—in 1936, the very year in which the Spanish Civil War broke out—programs of trade and economic cooperation with Germany. Moreover, this cooperation extended beyond commerce to military matters. Indeed, the Treaty of Rapallo, concluded back in 1922, initiated a long era of German-Soviet military cooperation by granting the Germans rights to establish military bases on Soviet territory. Germany used these to secretly create and test a host of weapons technologies prohibited by the Treaty of Versailles and also to conduct banned large-scale army maneuvers. By 1936, Soviet factories were being used to turn out German weapons. Through the hindsight of history, this appears to have been an act of national suicide, but, at the time, it was a great boon to Soviet industry, especially in the depths of worldwide economic depression.

To some degree, the cordiality of German-Soviet relations was kept secret, but the fact of trade and even much of the military cooperation could not be held entirely under wraps. Nevertheless, ideological apologists for Stalin and the many idealists who clung to the paradigm of absolute good (the political left) versus absolute evil (the political right) closed their eyes to reality and continued to accept Stalin as the pure champion of communism and the unyielding enemy of fascism and Nazism.

For his part, Stalin stood ready to deal with whatever side seemed to offer the best opportunity for Soviet survival and expansion. John Adams, champion of the American Revolution and second president of the United States, could not have known the word *Realpolitik* because it had yet to be coined, but he was himself a savvy practitioner of the art. To constitutional architect Roger Sherman of Connecticut, he wrote on July 18, 1789, "Power naturally grows." For Adams, that stark principle trumped all ideology. "Why? Because human passions are insatiable." And Adams went on to explain to Sherman his belief that the only way to keep power in check was to bring to bear an "equal power to control it." Only power could oppose, control, and manage power.

Unlikely as it seems, John Adams would have identified a political brother in Joseph Stalin, at least as far as the issue of power went. In 1935, Stalin and Molotov were negotiating in a conference at Moscow with France's premier Pierre Laval. In the course of the discussion, the Soviet leaders repeatedly probed Laval in a heavy-handed effort to ferret out information on the strength of the French army. Laval weaved and dodged, always endeavoring to change the subject. Winston Churchill, in volume one of his epic *Second World War* (1948), wrote about Laval ducking Stalin's question by asking one of his own: "'Can't you do something to encourage religion and the Catholics in Russia? It would help me so much with the Pope.'" Stalin's reply was swift: "'Oho! The Pope! How many divisions has *he* got?'" It was a retort both sarcastic and serious, a question born of real politics, the politics of power and of power countervailing power.

Casting his eye on the European situation of the 1930s, Stalin did not linger over the political words and ideological phrases that adorned the myriad banners that jarring mobs carried through the streets of great cities. Instead, he merely looked *through* these and asked the only question that mattered: *how many divisions?* When he saw Germany, Italy, and Japan creating the vaunted Axis, it was not their notions of fascism and Nazism that frightened him, it was the number of divisions they, together, could field against him—and, with Japan thrown into the mix, those divisions would be fielded on a two-front war, which Stalin wanted to avoid at all possible costs.

Turning to the Western democracies, primarily Britain and France, Stalin repeatedly offered the prospect of an anti-German defensive alliance, but was met with a combination of indifference (traumatized by the Great War of 1914–18, the people and politicians of France and Britain not only wanted to avoid war, they apparently wanted to avoid all talk of war, weapons, and military alliances) and outright distrust. For the latter, of course, there was ample reason. A leading doctrine of communism was the international

THE BEST OF ENEMIES

expansion of the Bolshevik Revolution, and, even if Stalin was not chiefly propelled by this ideology, he craved expansion for practical reasons. He wanted to amplify his own power in the form of acquiring buffer territories, political satellites that he could control as a bulwark against aggression from the West.

The Western democracies, invested in maintaining the post–World War I status quo as established by the Treaty of Versailles, did not want to facilitate Soviet expansion into the West. Thus, faced with a combination of indifference, distrust, and at least mild opposition from the likes of Britain and France, and also differing from these nations in point of diplomatic strategy—for the status quo was of no benefit to the Soviets—Stalin looked for an alliance with Germany.

In part, Joseph Stalin wanted to find a way to avoid having to fight Germany. In part, he wanted a genuine military alliance that would give him a piece of Poland and a controlling interest in the Baltic states. In part as well, he wanted to foment a war between Germany and the other Western powers—one in which the Soviet Union would do no more than play a spectator's role. Stalin hoped that Germany would fight France and Britain to the mutual exhaustion of all three, thereby leaving the Soviets in a relatively stronger position than any of them. It was all a matter of pitting power against power.

War between Germany and the West was, for Stalin, the best-case scenario he hoped to create with the nonaggression pact. Given the pacifist malaise into which the Western democracies had settled, in which appeasement rather than military threat was offered to counter Hitler's lust for conquest, Stalin began to realize that the war might be a long time coming, if at all. The democracies did not want to fight, and it looked as if they would give Hitler anything he wanted in order to avoid a fight. Nevertheless, striking a nonaggression deal with Hitler would buy the Soviet Union time to prepare itself for the major war that Stalin (and almost everyone else) believed would come sooner or later, whether with Germany, Japan, or the Western democracies.

Viewed from the perspective of Realpolitik, the Hitler-Stalin Pact seems eminently rational—amoral or downright immoral, perhaps, but certainly promising a host of pragmatic advantages for the Soviet Union. Yet no one ever accused Joseph Stalin of being invariably rational. Far from it. The 1930s saw the Moscow show trials and the Great Purge, a kind of latter-day Reign of Terror in which thousands were expelled from the Communist Party, many were executed, others were exiled, and, in the ranks of the army, three of five marshals, thirteen of fifteen army commanders, eight of nine admirals, fifty of fifty-seven army corps commanders, 154 out of 186 division commanders, all sixteen army commissars, and twenty-five of twenty-eight army corps commissars were purged, many of them put to death, rendering the Red Army especially vulnerable when Germany, unilaterally abrogating the Hitler-Stalin Pact, invaded the Soviet Union on June 22, 1941. Most of the world regarded the show trials and purges as truly insane, manifestations of Stalin's grandiose paranoia, but George Kennan, attached to the U.S. embassy in Moscow, studied the Moscow Trials closely and concluded that they actually "made some sense" when regarded as part of an overture to Hitler. To ideologues, Stalin advertised the trials as an effort to purge fascist infiltrators from the Communist Party and the Soviet government. To Hitler, however, it must also have been clear that Stalin was going out of his way to purge as many highly placed Jews as possible. Most prominent among the Jews ousted from the Soviet government was Foreign Minister Maxim Litvinov, who, during 1934–38, had campaigned (gallantly but with little success) in the League of Nations to rally an effective international resistance to the rise of Nazism. It was Litvinov who, in 1935, negotiated anti-German treaties with France and Czechoslovakia. Now, on May 3, 1939, Stalin summarily removed Litvinov as foreign minister, replacing him with Molotov. It was a signal to Hitler that the Soviet government was ready to negotiate, and Stalin sent Molotov to begin the process that quickly resulted in the German-Soviet nonaggression agreement. (While it is true that Litvinov was effectively purged, he was not subjected to trial. Indeed, after the German invasion of the Soviet Union in 1941, he was both vindicated and reinstated, serving as Soviet ambassador to the United States from November 1941 to August 1943, then recalled to the Soviet Union to become deputy commissar for foreign affairs. He achieved a goal denied many politicians, especially Jewish politicians, who rose during the era of Stalin. He died a natural death, in 1951.) If Kennan's insight is valid, Stalin was willing to sacrifice any number of key Party, government, and military figures in order to create the climate in which Hitler would agree to make an alliance with him.

IN REALPOLITIK, BARGAINING WITH THE DEVIL is nothing more or less than business as usual. One does what one must do. This does not alter the fact that the great liability of striking a bargain with the devil is that it is the devil with whom you are bargaining. Above all else, Satan is the Great Deceiver. A treaty is a contract, and even a contract concluded from the most pragmatic and opportunistic of motives carries with it an element of idealism in the form of an assumption of honor, the good-faith belief that both parties will attempt to live up to the agreement. Pragmatist though he was, Joseph Stalin believed in the contract he had signed, perhaps in much the same way as committed communists believed Stalin himself to be the unyielding champion of the ideology of the Bolshevik Revolution. In breaking his pact with Stalin, Adolf Hitler proved himself the greater pragmatist of the two. If ideology meant nothing to him, a contract stood for even less.

TAKEAWAY

IF ADHERENCE TO IDEOLOGY can conjure illusions born of naïve idealism, ruthless pragmatism—the practice of Realpolitik at its most extreme—tends to create an aura of invincibility, a confidence that one has broken free of all idealistic illusion and therefore has an unshakeable hold on bedrock reality. Play a game like RISK long enough and you are bound to encounter a ruthless player who makes alliances with the intention of breaking them. Such a player may win—if he gets a chance to play. But that may not happen very often. Few who know him want to give him a place at the game board. In the end, an alliance founded solely on power and position, concluded in the absence of character and principle, is so fragile as to be virtually nonexistent. One is a fool even to think of building a future on it.

CHAPTER 6

The Best of Allies

*The Roosevelt-Churchill
Partnership Begins*

∼✦∼

Previous page: *Detail of Franklin Delano Roosevelt and Winston Churchill at the Yalta Conference, February 1945.*

The Best of Allies

A T FIRST, FDR AND CHURCHILL didn't even like each other. It was July 1918, the United States was now in the "Great War," World War I, an ally of France and England, and thirty-six-year-old Franklin Delano Roosevelt was assistant secretary of the navy in the administration of Woodrow Wilson. His boss, Secretary of the Navy Josephus Daniels, sent him to survey the situation in Europe and, on July 29, young Roosevelt was invited to break bread in London at a banquet for the Allied ministers prosecuting the war. It was a night of rare summer beauty in the British capital, where, in the banqueting rooms of Gray's Inn, he met the former first lord of the Admiralty and present minister of munitions, forty-four-year-old Winston Spencer Churchill.

Franklin Roosevelt was slender and tall and, although he was a relatively young man, he affected old-fashioned pince-nez glasses, which did not so much make him look older as they gave him an air of pretension and even super-ciliousness. He did have a disarming habit of tossing his head whenever he wanted to make a point. Some found the gesture arrogant, others charming. He was accustomed to getting his way. Having been raised to rank and wealth on a Hudson River estate called Hyde Park, he was the son of a doting mother, who, while she exerted a great deal of control over him, denied him nothing. But if his mother had been a domineering presence in his early life, almost more influential was his beloved Groton School head-master, the Reverend Endicott Peabody, who had instilled in young Roosevelt a gospel of service. Wealth, Peabody told his students, brought with it a heavy debt to society, an obligation to create a better world. And, thus, from his youth, Roosevelt rejected a life of genteel leisure and embraced the spirit of public service and social reform that would inform his entire political career.

Like Roosevelt, Churchill had been born to privilege. His father, the Tory politician Lord Randolph Churchill, was descended from John Churchill, first duke of Marlborough, while his mother, the beautiful Jennie Jerome, was an American, daughter of a New York financier and horse-racing enthusiast. But whereas Roosevelt's father and mother were doting, neither of Churchill's parents showed their son much affection, and, after faring poorly in course work at Harrow, he entered the army via Sandhurst, Britain's preeminent military academy. Joining the 4th Hussars in 1895, Churchill took almost immediate leave to serve as a war correspondent during the Cuban war of independence. He then returned to his regiment in 1897 and saw service in India as a soldier and a journalist, producing his first book, *The Story of the Malakand Field Force*, the following year and a second, *The River War*, in 1899, after he had served with Lord Kitchener's Nile expeditionary force. That same year he resigned his commission, determined to enter politics and to support himself financially as a journalist and author. Defeated in his first parliamentary election, however, he took off for South Africa to report on the Second (Great) Boer War. Although a "mere" journalist, he participated in the heroic rescue of a British armored train, was captured by the Boers, and then reaped renown for his daring escape from them. His exploits helped win him a seat in Parliament in

1900, and, in the House of Commons, Churchill soon earned a reputation as a brilliant orator.

Up to this point, Churchill had been a Tory conservative, but he split with the party of his father in 1904 to become a Liberal and, as Roosevelt would be, an ardent social and labor reformer. It was Churchill who introduced an eight-hour day for miners, attacked so-called "sweated labor" practices in factories and workshops, and inaugurated a set of minimum wages as well as measures to reduce unemployment. Churchill's reforms brought charges that he was a traitor to his Tory class, much as FDR's lifelong advocacy of liberal causes and policies would draw criticism from moneyed conservatives in America. Yet the more opposition he faced, the more enthusiastically Churchill went about the business of reform, playing a key role in securing passage of the Parliament Act of 1911, which greatly curtailed the powers of the hereditary House of Lords, earned Churchill popular approval, and catapulted him to the cabinet office of home secretary. In this post, his Liberal zeal suddenly came up hard against reality. Faced with widespread strikes and labor violence, Churchill responded by repeatedly deploying the police, a policy that quickly undermined his hard-won Liberal credentials. At this time, he left the Home Office to become first lord of the Admiralty in October 1911. Like FDR, Churchill had a love of ships and naval matters. In the midst of a military crisis and arms race with Germany, he took steps to modernize the Royal Navy and ensure that it remained superior to the German fleet, so that the navy, far more than the British army, was prepared when World War I broke out in August 1914.

Like Churchill, Roosevelt was an advocate of naval preparedness, modernization, and expansion, although, as *assistant* secretary of the U.S. Navy, Roosevelt's authority was naturally far more limited than that of the first lord of the Admiralty.

For Churchill, the price of power proved high. After the first month of war, the Western Front became an entrenched stalemate, and, looking for a dramatic way out, Churchill proposed mounting an invasion across the Dardanelles strait to the Balkan peninsula called Gallipoli in order to open up direct communications with Russia on the Eastern Front. Strategically, the plan was bold; tactically, however, it was a costly disaster, which resulted in Churchill's removal as first lord of the Admiralty and, subsequently, his resignation from the government altogether in November 1915. He then fought on the Western Front as lieutenant colonel of the 6th Royal Scots Fusiliers, returning to Parliament in June 1916, and in July 1917, over Tory protest, he accepted appointment as minister of munitions. Thus, when he met Franklin Roosevelt at Gray's Inn, Churchill was a man of far greater experience than the younger American. He had reached the heights of power, and he had known the crushing weight of failure.

Franklin D. Roosevelt might have learned much from Winston Churchill that evening in 1918, but, in fact, the minister of munitions took almost no note of him, and, as late as 1939, speaking with his ambassador to Great Britain, Joseph P. Kennedy, President Roosevelt remarked: "I always disliked him since the time I went to England in 1917 or 1918. At a dinner I attended he acted like a stinker."

FDR's recollection was doubtless a distorted exaggeration, but there can be no doubt that the Gray's Inn dinner was for neither man an auspicious beginning to what would become one of the most important political relationships of the twentieth century and one of history's most momentous personal friendships. Yet it was not until after FDR had been inaugurated to his first term as president, in 1933, that Churchill, at this point nothing more than a mere member of Parliament and with very little power or influence, reached out. He sent the new president an inscribed copy of his latest book, the first volume of his magisterial *Marlborough: His Life and Times*. In his inscription, Churchill appealed to the social reformer in FDR. Making obvious reference to the commencement of the New Deal, he wrote: "With earnest best wishes for the success of the greatest crusade of modern times." It was a hearty but strange sentiment, coming as it did from a politician who, since his only encounter with Roosevelt, had once again become a Tory, a political conservative, many of whose beliefs and policies were now poles apart from the Progressive FDR.

Despite having been stricken and crippled by a paralytic illness in 1921 that left him unable to walk (long believed to have been polio, the disease was more likely Guillain-Barré syndrome), FDR rose to power during the 1920s, whereas Churchill's career during this same period shuttled wildly among journalism, history, and politics. Appointed by Prime Minister Stanley Baldwin, chancellor of the exchequer, the equivalent of secretary of the treasury, Churchill immediately put England back on the gold standard, which instantly triggered deflation, followed by widespread unemployment and a miners' strike that exploded into the nearly catastrophic nation-wide general strike of 1926. Churchill was vehemently unsympathetic to the strikers and, now widely perceived as the archenemy of labor, he withdrew from the Baldwin government in 1930 and took up a strident and reactionary campaign against a bill designed to give India the status of a self-governing dominion. Yet during the worst of the Great Depression, the "anti-labor" Churchill expressed admiration for FDR's pro-labor, even quasi-socialist New Deal, calling the American president "a bold fellow" in 1934 and remarking to the Oxford University Conservative Association, "I like his spirit."

The fact is that, by the late 1930s, although Roosevelt and Churchill had no personal or formal political relationship, they had much in common. Both were politicians and political leaders who anticipated war and who therefore advocated preparedness, but found themselves in a government and amid a public that so wanted to avoid armed conflict that they simply denied its possibility. In the United States, Congress passed a series of neutrality acts. In Britain, the government of Stanley Baldwin accelerated disarmament while willfully turning a blind eye to the Nazi program of arms build-up, and the government of Neville Chamberlain, which succeeded Baldwin, while admitting the wisdom of increased preparedness and rearmament, eagerly sought to "appease" Hitler by avoiding criticism of his naked aggression and giving him first part and then parcel of Czechoslovakia.

Like clear-eyed weathermen, both FDR and Churchill saw the war clouds gathering and refused to turn away from them. Roosevelt engineered passage of amendments and revisions to the neutrality legislation that, after the European war broke out in September 1939, transformed the still ostensibly neutral United States into the "arsenal of democracy," a supplier of munitions and *matériel* to the Allies. From the mid-1930s on, Churchill risked being condemned as a war-mongering Cassandra by incessantly sounding the warning in Parliament and relentlessly advocating preparedness. Exiled by Baldwin from the inner circles of government, Churchill nevertheless managed to obtain top-secret government intelligence on Germany's war buildup, particularly its air power. Indeed, with the help of a crusty Oxford physics professor named Frederick A. Lindemann, Churchill created something like a private intelligence service headquartered in his country estate, Chartwell, and produced information that was often far more accurate and extensive than what the government had. He injected this intelligence into his parliamentary speeches, warning of cataclysm if the German Luftwaffe overtook in strength the British Royal Air Force. Gradually, Churchill turned public and political opinion. Baldwin, while continuing to exclude Churchill from high office, nevertheless admitted him into the secret committee on air-defense research. Still, even Churchill was hesitant. When Mussolini's Italy invaded Ethiopia in 1935, he was torn. On the one hand, he wanted Britain to support a strong League of Nations response against the aggression, but on the other, he feared acting in a way that would propel the Italian dictator into the embrace of Adolf Hitler. The Spanish Civil War, which broke out in 1936, quickly became for fascist Italy and Nazi Germany a kind of surrogate war against the European democracies, yet Churchill, fearing to widen the conflict, at first supported the fascist Spanish militarist Francisco Franco.

Churchill's apparent vacillations really had the same purpose as Roosevelt's increasingly wary neutrality. Both men wanted to avoid provoking or widening war, but both sought to contain Nazi and fascist aggression and to prepare to fight it. By the time Neville Chamberlain succeeded Baldwin in 1937, Churchill had more sharply focused his message of warning, which caused the new prime minister to push him even farther away than Baldwin had.

The crisis came as Hitler pressed his demand for possession of the Sudetenland, the German-speaking portions of northern and western Bohemia and northern Moravia annexed to Czechoslovakia by the Treaty of Versailles after World War I. The population in this region was predominately ethnic German, and Hitler wanted it. Churchill urged Great Britain to make with France and the Soviets a joint declaration of purpose warning Hitler that any attempt to violate the sovereignty of Czechoslovakia would be met with force. Far from making such a declaration, however, Chamberlain met with Hitler at the Munich Conference of September 29-30, 1938, and concluded there the Munich Agreement, which gave the dictator all that he had asked for in exchange for his pledge to cease territorial expansion. This first fruit of the prime minister's "appeasement policy," Chamberlain declared, was "peace for our time." Churchill called it something else—"total and unmitigated defeat"—and agitated for a new coalition government that would return him to an office of national importance. Chamberlain resisted this, but, while he sparred with Churchill, Hitler, on March 16, 1939, repudiated his pledge to take no more territory and boldly marched his army into Prague. With this action, Czechoslovakia ceased to exist. What nation would fall next? The answer came swiftly.

At four in the morning of September 1, 1939, a vast German army and air force invaded Poland. Neville Chamberlain protested and gave warning. When Germany failed to respond and continued its invasion, the prime minister who had just months before announced "peace for our time," broadcast to the British nation on Sunday, September 3, at 11:15 in the morning the terrible fact that Great Britain was now at war with Germany. Later that very day, Chamberlain appointed Churchill first lord of the Admiralty, the same post he had occupied in World War I. Churchill was at the office by 6 P.M. that evening.

The American people eyed the European crisis with grave concern and high anxiety. Overwhelmingly, American public sentiment favored staying well out of this new world war.

On September 11, Franklin Roosevelt sent a letter to "My dear Churchill":

> It is because you and I occupied similar positions in the World War that I want you to know how glad I am that you are back again in the Admiralty. Your problems are, I realize, complicated by new factors but the essential is not very different. What I want you and the Prime Minister to know is that I shall at all times welcome it if

you will keep me in touch personally with anything
you want me to know about. You can always send
sealed letters through your [diplomatic] pouch or
my pouch.

The last two sentences must have given Churchill great
reason for hope. Certainly, they were not the words of a
leader bent on forever keeping his nation neutral. FDR
went on to acknowledge, apparently for the first time,
Churchill's gift of the Marlborough biography, the first
inscribed volume of which Churchill had sent the president back in 1933: "I am glad you did the Marlboro [sic]
volumes before this thing started—and I much enjoyed
reading them." He closed: "With my sincere regards,
Faithfully yours, Franklin D. Roosevelt." It was not an
entirely conventional closing, and we can only assume
that Churchill lingered hopefully over the words
"Faithfully yours."

By late autumn 1939, British insiders were predicting the
imminent fall of Neville Chamberlain and his replacement
by Winston Churchill. When this event actually came to pass
on May 10, 1940, the very day that Hitler's armies roared
into France, the Netherlands, Belgium, and Luxembourg,
FDR remarked to his cabinet that he "supposed Churchill
was the best man England had," then added: "even if he was
drunk half of the time." Those closer to the action were
even less confident. More than ever before, Ambassador
Joseph P. Kennedy was certain that Britain would fall, and
William C. Bullitt, U.S. ambassador to France, was of the
opinion that "there are no real leaders . . . in all of England
in this time of grave crisis."

It was in this climate of doubt that Roosevelt received Churchill's cable of May 15, 1940. It was his first to the president as prime minister, but Churchill insisted on identifying himself as "Former Naval Person," a wry insider joke, to underscore what each had in common with the other: the president the former undersecretary of the U.S. Navy, the prime minister the former first lord of the Admiralty. Churchill would use this form of self-identification throughout the entire war. "Although I have changed my office," Churchill began, "I am sure you would not wish me to discontinue our intimate, private correspondence." They were curious, bold adjectives, expressing Churchill's hopes rather than accurately describing a relationship that, at this point, hardly even existed.

Churchill had made his first stirring speech to Parliament two days before he cabled Roosevelt. He repeated to the House what he "said to those who have joined this government: 'I have nothing to offer but blood, toil, tears and sweat.'" To President Roosevelt he now reported on the war just as unflinchingly: Air attacks are "making a deep impression upon the French," and the "small countries are simply smashed up, one by one, like matchwood. . . . We expect to be attacked here ourselves, both from the air and by parachute and air-borne troops. . . . If necessary, we shall continue the war alone and we are not afraid of that. But I trust you realise, Mr. President, that the voice and force of the United States may count for nothing if they are withheld too long. You may have a completely subjugated, Nazified Europe established with astonishing swiftness, and the weight may be more than we can bear."

Churchill was both realistic and resolute, neither crying nor raising a cry of war. To the American president who had come into office in 1933 telling the American people that the only force they needed to fear was fear itself, Churchill said "we are not afraid," and he asked for a U.S. proclamation of nonbelligerency, "which would mean that you would help us with everything short of actually engaging armed forces." It was a notch up from absolute neutrality. Nonbelligerency meant that America could provide noncombatant support to Britain. The prime minister asked for forty or fifty obsolescent World War I–vintage American destroyers (desperately needed to escort British convoys), several hundred new aircraft, anti-aircraft defense equipment, and steel. He also requested that a U.S. Navy squadron be dispatched to visit an Irish port to discourage what was believed to be an impending landing in neutral Ireland by German paratroopers, and he suggested that FDR send warships to Singapore, "to keep that Japanese dog quiet in the Pacific." Germany's ally Japan had not yet declared war on Britain. Churchill concluded by unabashedly extending his "hand" cupped palm up: "We shall go on paying dollars for as long as we can, but I should like to feel reasonably sure that when we can pay no more, you will give us the stuff all the same."

Despite the tone of the cable, Roosevelt, who replied on May 17, was wary. He demurred on the request for destroyers and planes by pointing out that only Congress could authorize such aid, and promising to think about sending ships to Ireland, but advising Churchill that he would keep the Pacific fleet in Pearl Harbor at least "for the time being."

In his reply the very next day, Churchill put the best face on the president's communication but also increased the pressure on him: "Many thanks for your message for which I am grateful. I do not need to tell you about the gravity of what has happened. We are determined to persevere to the very end whatever the result of the great battle raging in France may be. We must expect in any case to be attacked here . . . before very long and we hope to give a good account of ourselves. But if American assistance is to play any part it must be available [soon]."

Recent historians, especially Jon Meacham, in his 2003 book *Franklin and Winston: An Intimate Portrait of an Epic Friendship,* have made much of the way Churchill cultivated a personal friendship with Roosevelt in order to build a full-fledged Anglo-American alliance. While it is true that the prime minister exercised his charm on the American president, what first unmistakably drew Roosevelt to Churchill's side was not the prime minister's personal communications to him, but his public performance. The British leader's stance was heroic and defiant, yet realistic. His speeches to the British people—which, via broadcast, Churchill knew would be heard by America and the whole world—were sublimely inspirational and sublimely realistic: "Our task is not only to win the battle, but to win the war. . . . [T]he long night of barbarism will descend unbroken by even a star of hope, unless we conquer—as conquer we must—as conquer we shall."

Yet even as Churchill voiced his certainty that Britain would conquer, France was falling to Hitler, and the British troops there, the bulk of Britain's professional army, were being pushed toward the English Channel at a place called Dunkirk. From London, Ambassador Kennedy sent the president a cable on May 27, 1940: "Only a miracle can save the BEF [British Expeditionary Force] from being wiped out or, as I said yesterday, surrender." He went on to say that the possibility, even the desirability, of British surrender was in the air. Whereas Churchill and a few others "want to fight to the death . . . other members [of the Cabinet] realize that physical destruction of men and property in England will not be a proper offset to a loss of pride."

FDR by now knew his ambassador was a defeatist, yet, given the scale of desperation in Europe, how could he possibly credit Churchill's perception of reality more than Kennedy's? Besides, FDR had public opinion polls indicating that a mere 7.7 percent of Americans favored entering the war now and just 19 percent thought entry would be justified even if Allied defeat looked imminent. Now was no time to lobby Congress to get into the war, yet the president continued to offer hope for the future, writing "You are much in my thoughts. I need not tell you that."

What neither FDR nor Ambassador Kennedy knew was that, on May 26, the miracle the ambassador mentioned had already begun. Using a motley assortment of warships, merchant ships, fishing vessels, yachts, and, indeed, anything that floated, the British had begun evacuating Dunkirk. By the time the operation ended, on June 4, more than 300,000 BEF and some 38,000 French and other troops had been saved. On that very day, Churchill delivered to the House of Commons perhaps his most famous speech:

We shall fight on the beaches, we shall fight on the landing grounds, we shall fight in the fields and in the streets, we shall fight in the hills; we shall never surrender, and even if, which I do not for a moment believe, this island or a large part of it were subjugated and starving, then our Empire beyond the seas, armed and guarded by the British fleet, would carry on the struggle, until, in God's good time, the new world, with all its power and might, steps forth to the rescue and the liberation of the old.

FDR seemed to get the message. On June 10, the day Italy declared war on England and France, the president gave the commencement address to the University of Virginia Law School Class of 1940:

In our American unity, we will pursue two obvious and simultaneous courses: we will extend to the opponents of force the material resources of this nation; and, at the same time, we will harness and speed up the use of those resources in order that we ourselves in the Americas may have equipment and training equal to the task of any emergency and every defense. Signs and signals call for speed—full speed ahead.

Churchill, who heard the speech broadcast, cabled the president on June 11: "We all listened to you last night and were fortified by the grand scope of your declaration. Your statement that the material aid of the United States will be given to the Allies in their struggle is a strong encouragement in a dark but not unhopeful hour." Next, Churchill was thrilled when FDR sent Prime Minister Paul Reynaud of France a telegram promising aid and expressing America's "faith in and . . . support for the ideals for which the Allies are fighting." Yet when Churchill urged Roosevelt to make the telegram public, the president refused, not wanting to appear to be taking a step toward actually declaring war. The prime minister's spirits fell, and France surrendered to Germany on June 22, 1940.

Britain was now alone indeed. Shortly after the fall of France, the U.S. departments of War and the Navy advised the president that sending more *matériel* to Britain would serve only to "weaken our present state of defense." Yet Roosevelt, without committing the nation to war, kept supplying whatever he felt could be spared. In the meantime, during July, FDR decided to stop relying on secondhand assessments of the British situation, especially assessments originating with the dubious Joseph P. Kennedy. Instead, he sent to London Colonel "Wild Bill" Donovan, the man who would create the Americans' key wartime intelligence agency, the Office of Strategic Services (OSS). Donovan painted a surprisingly hopeful picture of British prospects, and, clearly, it was just what Roosevelt wanted to hear. Yet, in the middle of an election year, running for an unprecedented third term against Republican Wendell Wilkie, who pledged that "no American boys will ever be sent to the shambles of the European trenches," FDR continued to withhold full commitment.

Churchill had been dealt both hope and disappointment at the hands of Franklin Roosevelt, but he always chose to seize on the hope, and now he was anxious, more anxious than FDR himself, about the outcome of the election. Even during the reelection campaign, in September, Roosevelt made bold to push through at long last a destroyers-for-bases deal, whereby the United States would give Britain fifty obsolescent destroyers in return for the use of British naval bases in the Western hemisphere. But he held off, until after the election, taking the next step, which would be known as Lend-Lease, the policy of supplying *matériel* to the Allies without cash payment. Anxious as he was for the stuff of war, Churchill, a politician as well as a prime minister, understood, and when FDR defeated Wilkie, Churchill dispatched a cable on the day after the victory: "I feel you will not mind my saying that I prayed for your success and that I am truly thankful for it." Yet he took care to avoid pressing the reelected president too hard. Thankfulness for Roosevelt's victory did "not mean that I seek or wish for anything more than the full, fair and free play of your mind upon the world issues now at stake in which our two nations have to discharge their respective duties," he wrote, adding: "Things are afoot which will be remembered as long as the English language is spoken in any quarter of the globe, and in expressing the comfort I feel that the people of the United States have once again cast these great burdens upon you, I must avow my sure faith that the lights by which we steer will bring us all safely to anchor."

Roosevelt never replied to the prime minister's note of congratulation, even after Churchill cabled ten days later: "I hope you got my personal telegram of congratulation."

Yet, with the election won, FDR quickly advanced to the concept of Lend-Lease, which was enacted by Congress on March 11, 1941.

Roosevelt understood—and was at pains to make the American people understand—that England's survival, especially as a great naval power, was an essential safeguard to the security of the United States. True, America was an ocean away from Germany, but it was chiefly the Royal Navy that defended that ocean. Wisely, FDR sold the Lend-Lease concept to Congress and the public as a purely selfish move, intended not so much to help England as to defend America. Yet, as he remarked to his long-time advisor and confidant Harry Hopkins, he needed to get closer to Churchill: "a lot . . . could be settled if Churchill and I could just sit down together for a while." Politically and diplomatically, this seemed impossible at the moment because it would appear as if the president were moving headlong into an outright alliance. Hopkins solved the political dilemma by volunteering to visit Churchill on his behalf.

When the visit was first proposed, Churchill had never heard of Harry Hopkins, but as soon as he learned that this man was as good as the president's own eyes and ears and was deeply devoted to FDR, he ladied on flattery of Hopkins's boss, praising him in a speech on January 9, 1941, the day before he was scheduled to meet with Hopkins at Downing Street. Churchill lauded the American president as "a famous statesman, long versed and experienced in the work of government and administration, in whose heart there burns the fire of resistance to aggression and oppression, and whose sympathies and nature make him the sincere and undoubted champion of justice and freedom, and of the victims of wrongdoing wherever they may dwell." Thus the prime minister got off on the right foot, and Hopkins, observing him in action over the next few weeks, reported to the president: "*Churchill is the gov't in every sense of the word,*" and he went on to an unambiguous conclusion: "This island needs our help now Mr. President with everything we can give them." At dinner with Churchill in Scotland, Hopkins addressed the prime minister: "I suppose you wish to know what I am going to say to President Roosevelt on my return. Well, I'm going to quote you one verse from that Book of Books . . . : 'Whither thou goest, I will go; and where thou lodgest, I will lodge: thy people shall be my people, and thy God my God.'" He paused, then added: "'Even to the end.'"

At this, Winston Churchill wept.

On January 19, 1941, the president handed his recent rival, Wendell Wilkie, who was about to leave for England, a note to give the prime minister. Its substance consisted of verses FDR had committed to memory from Longfellow's "The Building of the Ship":

I think this verse applies to your people as it does to us.

> Sail on, O Ship of State!
> Sail on, O Union, strong and great!
> Humanity with all its fears,
> With all the hopes of future years,
> Is hanging breathless on thy fate!
>
> As ever yours,
> Franklin D. Roosevelt

The "ship of state," as it turned out, was more literal than metaphoric. Early Sunday evening, August 3, 1941, FDR embarked on the presidential yacht *Potomac* for what was billed as a few days of fishing. At dawn two days later, off Martha's Vineyard and in absolute secrecy, the president and a small party were transferred from the *Potomac* to the U.S. Navy cruiser *Augusta,* which steamed toward Placentia Bay, Newfoundland, and a rendezvous with the British warship H.M.S. *Prince of Wales.* Aboard her was Prime Minister Winston Churchill. The secrecy was crucial for two reasons. A majority of Congress and a majority of the people of the United States were still fearful of being drawn closer to the embattled British, and FDR did not want to make them any more nervous before he actually met with Churchill. More important, the Atlantic Ocean was a very dangerous place, with German surface raiders and U-boats regularly sinking thousands of tons of British shipping. If it were even suspected that the prime minister was crossing the ocean, no ship would escape targeting.

The *Augusta* and the *Prince of Wales* drew toward one another as August 9 dawned over the deceptively peaceful bay. At about eleven, Churchill boarded a launch and motored across the bay to the anchored American ship. Dressed in the dark blue uniform of a Royal Navy officer, the prime minister clambered aboard and faced the president of the United States, who stood, in the suit of a civilian, leaning on the arm of his son Elliott, the heavy steel braces that supported him hidden beneath his trouser legs. The two men stood facing each other as the national anthems of both nations were played.

As they looked toward one another, President Roosevelt must have been keenly aware of the great risk Churchill had taken in making the trip. For his part, the prime minister had a deep and sympathetic admiration for the personal courage of a chief executive who insisted on standing, painfully supported by braces on the rising and falling deck of a ship at anchor.

The anthems concluded, Churchill stepped forward, bowed slightly, and presented Roosevelt with a letter from King George VI. Extending his hand, the president said, "At last—we've gotten together."

"We have," Churchill nodded.

The pair lunched. Harry Hopkins, who was present at the meal, remarked on their almost instant rapport, even though Churchill had completely forgotten having met Roosevelt at Gray's Inn, back in 1918, during the first war.

If, as Jon Meacham and other historians have argued, a kind of "courtship" between prime minister and president began aboard the *Augusta*, it would not always go smoothly—though never for lack of trying on Churchill's part. For him, it would never be enough to have the United States as a political and military ally. He wanted the nation's leader as an intimate friend on whom he could depend in a personal way. A successful politician, Churchill knew all about the dangers of wearing your heart on your sleeve, but, with FDR, he would do precisely this almost all of the time. Roosevelt, however, would never fully reveal the heart behind his politics. To the people of the United States, FDR seemed all at once a brother, a father, an uncle, and a friend. He had brought America through the Great Depression with Fireside Chats that seemed personally directed to each and every listener. To radiate warmth and confidence, he needed only to flash his magnificent smile, toss back his head, or angle his long, slender cigarette holder even more jauntily. Yet those who knew him better, who worked with him daily, found something cooler and more remote in the president. Publicly self-confident, genial, and indefatigable in his optimism, FDR always held something back on a person-to-person level. Harry S. Truman thought him both "a great man" and an "old fakir." Others, who knew him well enough to know that they never could really get to know him, simply described Franklin Delano Roosevelt as a *politician* from start to finish. Whereas Churchill felt an imperative to form a bond of personal friendship with the New World leader, FDR's goal was not so much to make a friend of the prime minister as it was to charm him, the way a politician charms all of his leading constituents. There was a willingness on Churchill's part to make himself emotionally vulnerable. Roosevelt, perhaps because his physical state made him perpetually vulnerable, showed no such willingness. Nevertheless, while the relationship between the two leaders was unequal from the start, it was always personal, first and foremost, and this remains a most remarkable fact.

In August 1941, Britain obviously needed the United States. Less obvious to many was America's need of Britain, but, already, FDR was working to make that need clear to the American people. "The best immediate defense of the United States," he said at a press conference on December 17, 1940, "is the success of Great Britain defending itself." He explained that "from a selfish point of view of American defense . . . we should do everything to help the British Empire to defend itself." Yet military necessity and political advantage were never enough for either Churchill or Roosevelt. In this unprecedented crisis engulfing or threatening to engulf the entire world, these two men—in different degrees—felt the need for something more personal.

As a result of the "Atlantic Conference" aboard the two nations' warships, the leaders concluded the Atlantic Charter, which they signed on August 14, agreeing on a set of common political and more broadly philosophical principles, including the necessity of Nazi defeat. The Atlantic Conference concluded, Franklin Roosevelt returned to a peaceful nation on the verge of war, and Churchill to a nation already at war and very possibly on the verge of annihilation. Roosevelt came back having made an unpopular pledge of alliance just short of combat, while Churchill returned with what was probably an inflated estimate of what that pledge meant and, in consequence, an exaggerated feeling of optimism as Britain continued to make its way through its darkest hours.

Then followed one of Roosevelt's own darkest hours. On September 7, 1941, his mother died. Always an equal mixture of love and smothering concern, Sara Roosevelt had been Franklin's only parent since his eighteenth year when his father died. Churchill tore himself from the war room at 10 Downing Street to send a cable: "Pray accept my deep sympathy in your most grievous loss." To which the president replied immediately with thanks "for your kind and friendly message." Just four days later, FDR broadcast a Fireside Chat to the nation regarding German U-boat attacks, including a recent bombing of the American destroyer USS *Greer* on September 4:

We have sought no shooting war with Hitler. . . .
But when you see a rattlesnake poised to strike,
you do not wait until he has struck before you
crush him. . . . From now on, if German or Italian
vessels of war enter the waters, the protection of
which is necessary for American defense, they do
so at their own peril.

Having heard the broadcast, Churchill wrote to a friend:
"As we used to sing at Sandhurst 'Now we *shan't* be long!'"

In the Atlantic, an undeclared naval war between the
United States and Germany now heated up, and the prepa-
rations for war that FDR had begun with successive
modifications to the Neutrality Acts, the institution of
Lend-Lease, and the commencement of the first peacetime
military draft in American history took on increasing
urgency. But the decisive blow would fall an ocean away, on
December 7, 1941, when Germany's ally Japan bombed
Pearl Harbor in the United States territory of Hawaii.

The blow was devastating: three battleships were sunk
(including the obsolete *Utah*) and six damaged (three
severely, three less badly, all salvageable); three destroyers,
three light cruisers, and four other ships also went down.
The Japanese planes destroyed 164 U.S. aircraft on the
ground and damaged another 128. In all, 2,388 soldiers,
sailors, and civilians were killed, and 1,174 were wounded.

The instant he heard the news of the attack over the
radio, Churchill, whose nation was fighting for its life
against Germany, resolved to declare war on Japan as well.
John "Gil" Winant, the American ambassador who had
replaced Joseph P. Kennedy, cautioned the prime minister

that he couldn't "declare war on a radio announcement," and told Churchill that he would "call up the President by telephone and ask him what the facts are." Churchill asked to speak to FDR as well. After making the connection and talking with the president for a time, Winant handed the receiver to Churchill, saying to FDR, "You will know who it is as soon as you hear his voice."

"Mr. President, what's this about Japan?"

"It's quite true. They have attacked us at Pearl Harbor. We are all in the same boat now."

In one stroke, the United States Pacific fleet had been decimated, and the nation plunged into war. It is a testament to how Churchill felt about Roosevelt that he did not dissemble his feelings about the event with conventional exclamations of shock and claims of condolence. What he said was: "This certainly simplifies things." And, more quietly, closed with: "God be with you."

Several years after the war, Churchill wrote in *The Second World War* (Volume III): "to have the United States at our side was to me the greatest joy. I could not foretell the course of events. . . . but now at this very moment I knew the United States was in the war, up to the neck and in to the death. So we had won after all!" Pearl Harbor was for Japan both a tactical triumph and a strategic catastrophe. The Pacific fleet reeled, but it was the Empire of Japan that, as a result of the attack, would finally fall, and, even sooner, Japan's ally, Germany would be reduced to rubble and ruin.

As any RISK PLAYER KNOWS, playing the game with a friend adds to the intensity and quality of the contest. Thanks to the strategic friendship forged by Roosevelt and Churchill, England no longer faced its enemies alone—and neither did the United States. Throughout the war, the two national leaders would continually communicate by cable and frequently meet in person. They would formulate war aims and war strategy together, creating a victorious partnership uniquely compounded of military necessity, global vision, and intimate personal friendship.

TAKEAWAY

NEVER IN MODERN HISTORY—perhaps never in all of history—has so vast, costly, and consequential an alliance between nations depended on so truly strategic a friendship, driven and guided by the goodwill and genuine affection of one human being for another. Yet it is crucially important to place equal emphasis on the word "strategic" as well as "friendship." Neither motive—strategic advantage nor friendly affection—can be allowed to assume absolute dominance in a truly productive alliance. It is the balanced presence of both that unquestionably increases the productivity of a high-stakes alliance.

CHAPTER 7

Ike and the Admiral

*How the Supreme Allied Commander
Turned a Traitor into an Asset*

∽∾∽

Ike and the Admiral

THE JAPANESE "SNEAK ATTACK" on Pearl Harbor, December 7, 1941, ignited in the American people a burning desire for instant vengeance. The strategic reality of a two-front global war, however, dictated that the United States focus most aggressively first on the struggle against Hitler and Mussolini in Europe while fighting a holding action against Japan in the Pacific. President Franklin D. Roosevelt and the U.S. high command were agreed on this strategy, but both army chief of staff General George C. Marshall and the commander he put in charge of U.S. forces being sent across the Atlantic, General Dwight D. "Ike" Eisenhower, wanted to move even more aggressively and more quickly in Europe. They proposed a virtually immediate invasion of the continent, jumping off from England across the English Channel to France. Britain's Prime Minister Winston Churchill and his high command, while thankful that Ike and Marshall were willing to address the European front before devoting full resources to the Pacific, nevertheless countered that such an attempt at an invasion of the mainland would be premature, that neither the British nor American forces were ready for it. Instead, Churchill advocated that the Allies' first offensive should not be in Europe at all, but in North Africa, from which they could then invade Europe via the Mediterranean, attacking what the prime minister liked to call the continent's "soft underbelly." Very grudgingly, Marshall and Eisenhower acquiesced, and despite their lukewarm attitude toward what was now code-named Operation Torch, the Anglo-American landings in French

Morocco and Algeria would be primarily a U.S. show under Eisenhower's direction.

Strategic territories in North Africa were occupied by the Germans and Italians, but, in addition to them, there was a wildcard force, the Vichy French. Early in the war, in June 1940, with German forces having overrun France, the popular hero of World War I, Henri-Philippe Pétain, assumed the French premiership and led the government to solicit surrender terms from Germany. On June 22, a humiliating armistice was concluded, the terms of which allowed France the charade of semi-sovereignty by dividing the country into an unoccupied southern zone (with a capital at Vichy—and therefore known as Vichy France) and a German-occupied northern and western coastal zone. France's colonial possessions in North Africa, including Morocco and Algeria, were part of the unoccupied Vichy zone. By the approach of Operation Torch in the fall of 1942, it had become clear that Vichy had no real authority over the destiny of the French people and was, in fact, nothing more than a German puppet regime. The last vestige of something approaching genuine sovereignty, however, was found in North Africa, and Eisenhower could only hope that the Vichy leaders and forces there would either side with the Allies or, at least, offer no substantial resistance.

Beginning with Algeria and French Morocco, Operation Torch was to be the first step in carrying out the overall mission assigned to Eisenhower, to conquer all of Axis-occupied North Africa, but it was to be more than just a first step. It was to be the American army's baptism of fire. As Ike was keenly aware, Germany and Italy would be sufficiently formidable adversaries without the untested Americans having to deal with the French as well.

The Torch landings were scheduled for November 8, 1942, and to feel out the Vichy, Eisenhower sent one of his top subordinates, Major General Mark W. Clark—the tall, aquiline figure Churchill called "an American eagle"—to make a hazardous covert landing near Algiers on October 21 to meet with Vichy Major General Charles Mast, chief of staff of the French XIX Corps, a man Ike and his intelligence advisors believed to have pro-Allied sympathies. Clark managed to negotiate from Mast a pledge that, given four days' notice of the landings, he would ensure that the French army and air force would offer no more than token resistance—a mere "demonstration" he said was necessary to appease French military honor. This pledge, however, entirely left out the French navy, on behalf of which, Mast explained, he could not speak, let alone make any guarantees.

Mast's promise was a thin thread indeed, but Eisenhower believed it was better than nothing. He proceeded with the planning and implementation of Operation Torch on the assumption that French resistance would be light, although he warned his commanders to be prepared for the worst. The November 8 invasion consisted of three landings: at the Moroccan metropolis of Casablanca and at the Algerian cities of Oran and Algiers. Total Allied troop strength of the landings was 65,000, slightly more than half the strength of the Vichy French forces in North Africa. If, therefore, the French chose to resist in earnest, the badly outnumbered Allies would have a most difficult time and might even be driven back, doubtless with heavy losses.

As it turned out, Mast's pledge proved good in Algiers and Oran, the first place offering no resistance, the second putting up a token struggle and falling on the second day of the operation. At Casablanca, French resistance was much stiffer, but, on November 10, the principal French authority in North Africa, Admiral François Darlan, agreed to order a general ceasefire, and Casablanca accordingly capitulated on November 11.

Eisenhower learned all he could about Darlan, who, he believed, was the key figure controlling the Vichy government and its military assets in North Africa as well as the chief colonial authority to whom the native population answered. Strike a deal with him, control him, and the French could be permanently turned from potential adversaries to allies—or, at the very least, noncombatants. In contrast to some other Vichy commanders, who regarded the Nazis as invaders, Darlan had welcomed the Germans and had been an enthusiastic leader of the French-Nazi collaboration. An admiral in the French navy, he had served as Pétain's deputy premier in the Vichy government. In the 1930s, as war clouds gathered, the right-wing admiral frequently vented his anti-English sentiments and, when the Battle of France got under way in the spring of 1940, he publicly expressed his hope that Germany would win the war. After Pétain formally concluded the armistice with the Nazis on June 22, 1940, Darlan dispatched the formidable French fleet to colonial bases in North Africa and ordered all officers and sailors to conduct themselves with absolute loyalty to Vichy. In February 1941, Darlan became vice premier and was even anointed by the aging Pétain as his successor. At this same time, Darlan became minister for foreign affairs, defense, and the interior, and in January 1942 was appointed commander in chief of French armed forces and the high commissioner for North Africa.

Had Ike stopped his analysis of Admiral Darlan here, he could not have expected much from negotiating with him. To all appearances, the admiral was a traitor, period. But Ike looked more closely and peered beneath the surface of appearance. He knew that Adolf Hitler had feared the concentration of so many offices and so much authority in one man, and, accordingly, had pressed Darlan to yield his cabinet posts to another leading collaborationist, Pierre Laval, on April 17, 1942. Ike reasoned that Darlan would not be likely to believe that Hitler, who had taken power *from* him, regarded him as anything approaching a full partner in conquest. Ike saw Darlan as a man driven by self-interest, and Darlan's self-interest is precisely what Hitler had failed to satisfy. For this reason, Ike believed he had found an opening, a way to flip Darlan.

He was right. When the Torch landings came, on November 8, Darlan immediately entered into negotiations with the Allies, agreeing to the November 10 ceasefire and surrendering altogether the following day. Eisenhower could have deposed and disposed of Darlan right then and there. Certainly, that is what the gallant Free French nationalists, led by Charles de Gaulle, wanted him to do. But, acting on his own authority, Ike boldly decided to offer an alliance so controversial that it might well have cost him his command. He secured from Darlan an agreement to cooperate fully with the Allies in return for Eisenhower's official confirmation and approval of his position as the chief civil and military administrator of French North Africa. In return for his cooperation, Eisenhower promised to keep Darlan in power.

Predictably, de Gaulle was outraged, as was the French Resistance and even many among the British and American public. There were strident calls for Eisenhower's removal, but both President Roosevelt and Prime Minister Churchill stood behind Ike. In a letter to his son, John S. D. Eisenhower, on December 20, Eisenhower explained, "Apparently, the people who have been creating the storm [of protest] do not like Darlan. The answer to that one is 'Who does?'"

There was no sugarcoating it. Darlan *was* a traitor, and he was therefore a dangerous man, but, at this particular time and in this particular place, he represented authority, not only over the Vichy forces in the region, but over large segments of the native population. "It is important," Eisenhower wrote to Mark Clark, "that we do not create any dissension among the tribes or encourage them to break away from existing methods of control." The last thing Ike wanted to do was to fight the French, the native North Africans, *and* the Germans and Italians. "To organize this country in support of the war effort, we must use French officials and we do not want any internal unrest or trouble."

Distasteful? Absolutely. Not only was Darlan a treacherous leader with strong, avowed, and demonstrated fascist and Nazi sentiments, the French colonial officials who answered to him were hardly selfless or unified in their own agendas. They were, many of them, notoriously corrupt, and this was for Eisenhower a rich source of anger and frustration. Nevertheless, he did not allow his personal feelings to interfere with his overriding objective: to take the Vichy forces out of the war and to ensure the cooperative neutrality of the natives. Toward this end, he would go to any lengths. Doubtless Ike held his nose when he ordered Clark to "Give them some money if it will help." Although Ike was unwilling to compromise on the objective of victory, he was very much willing to make certain ethical compromises to achieve that objective. Francs and dollars, after all, were far cheaper than bullets and blood.

There is no pleasure in dealing with people who had proven themselves dishonorable, as Ike rightly believed the Vichy officers had. Moreover, it was nearly impossible to determine from day to day where each Vichy official stood, as the ranks of the colonial officers were rife with nervous opportunists. Yet it seemed clear to Eisenhower that the fastest, surest, and most economical route to total victory lay through a series of compromises, including even outright bribery. Sometimes, strategic alliances require a difficult combination of flexibility and rigidity and the ability to decide exactly where and when to bend and where and when to remain absolutely unbending.

As for the storm of criticism Ike's Darlan decision unleashed, he pointed out to his son that, "at the moment of crisis," he was confident he had made both the "right and just" decision. "That is one reason we train people all their lives to be soldiers, so that in a moment of emergency they can get down to the essentials of the situation and not be too much disturbed about popularity or newspaper acclaim."

It was and always is a very risky business. The "right and just" decision may or may not be the most popular decision. It could even put your job in jeopardy. Moreover, a decision made in a moment of crisis might, in the fullness of time, prove to be a bad decision, the wrong decision. Yet, in a crisis, the overriding imperative is to make a decision. In a crisis, the failure to decide almost always has graver consequences than making a less-than-perfect or even a wrong decision. And one thing a crisis does not allow for is the taking of a public opinion poll or the convening of a focus group.

After securing Darlan's cooperation, Ike also worked to establish amicable relations with the admiral's right-hand man in the army, General Auguste Noguès, a figure so given to waffling between sides that Allied troops modified his name to "General No-Yes." Ike's approach to him and to the other French commanders was to create common cause, to make Darlan, Noguès, and the others at least *feel* that they were his partners in the conduct of military and civil operations. In this, Ike effectively lifted a leaf from Hitler's own book with regard to the entire Vichy charade. But he did it with a much lighter touch. For example, to Noguès, on November 15, Eisenhower wrote asking that the general "bring to my early attention any instances in which you consider that any part of the forces under my command are failing to contribute their full share in producing the amity and cooperation you and I are seeking." Look closely at the language. Ike invited Noguès to alert him to failures among *Allied* officers and enlisted men, thereby accepting full personal responsibility for correcting any problems. But note that he also emphasized that the objective was a shared one (the italics have been added): "the amity and cooperation *you and I* are seeking."

He continued: "I know you are animated by the same impulses [that animate me]."

Not that Eisenhower actually believed that he and Vichy commanders could ever truly be partners "animated by the same impulses." But he said what he thought he had to say in order to secure their cooperation. As he explained in a secret cable to his aide, Lieutenant General Walter Bedell "Beetle" Smith, on November 18, 1942, in dealing with Darlan and Noguès, he was not acting the part of "kingmaker," as his many critics accused, but was "simply trying to get a complete and firm military grip on North Africa, which I was sent down here to do." His only objective, he explained to Smith, was to "get Tunisia quickly," so that the Axis—Germany and Italy—would not have "time to do as it pleases in that region," including inciting fascist Spain to abandon its neutrality and openly join its cause. "The potential consequences of delay are enormous," he warned Smith, "because this battle is not, repeat not yet won." Ike assured Smith that he did "not expect any encouragement and hurrahs from the rear, but I regret that I must use so much of my own time to keep explaining these matters."

THE UNPLEASANT, UNPOPULAR, AND UNEASY ALLIANCE Dwight Eisenhower forged with men he considered traitors bought time and saved blood. It hastened victory in North Africa, even at the cost of his having to endure and fend off bitter criticism both from the public and such

Allied leaders as Charles de Gaulle. Added to the disagreeable business of partnering with those he neither respected nor trusted, Eisenhower also had to devote time to persuading those above him to trust his judgment and his motives and simply to let him do his job.

TAKEAWAY

WHETHER IN RISK OR REAL LIFE, you don't have to like or respect your ally. You just need to have a good idea of how far you can trust him. Dancing with the devil is never a pleasure or an honor, but sometimes the devil is the only partner you can find.

CHAPTER 8

The General and the Physicist

*Groves and Oppenheimer Build
an Atomic Bomb*

∽∾∾

Previous page: *Leslie Groves and J. Robert Oppenheimer in an undated photograph.*

The General and the Physicist

BUILDING AN "ATOMIC BOMB"? It was not even a job he wanted.

The son of a U.S. Army chaplain, Leslie Richard Groves was a hard-driving engineer and career military officer, as brilliant as he was irascible and opportunistic. Educated at the University of Washington and MIT before he enrolled in West Point, Groves graduated from the academy in 1918, fourth in his class, and was commissioned in the branch of the service reserved for the best and brightest of the Point's graduates, the Army Corps of Engineers. After taking advanced courses at the army's Engineer's School during 1918–20 and again in 1921, he worked on major military construction projects in San Francisco, Hawaii, Delaware, and Nicaragua, before he was assigned in 1931 to the Office of the Chief of Engineers in Washington, D.C. From here, he was soon tapped for enrollment in the Command and General Staff School at Fort Leavenworth, Kansas, from which he graduated in 1936, and, while still a lowly captain, was sent to the Army War College, an institution reserved for those who had been earmarked by their superiors for the highest levels of command. After graduating from the War College in 1939, Groves was assigned to the General Staff in Washington, received rapid promotion to major and then temporary colonel, and in 1940 was assigned first to the Office of the Quartermaster General and then again to the Office of the Chief of Engineers. Here he was given the single biggest engineering assignment the army had to offer: supervision of the construction of the Pentagon, just outside of Washington, D.C.

Promotion in the U.S. Army between the wars proceeded at a notoriously glacial pace. Groves's rise, however, had been meteoric, and that did not please everyone. Many of his colleagues and contemporaries viewed Leslie Groves as a cold careerist, hyper-ambitious, even ruthless. Worst of all, he didn't much care what others thought of him. He had no need to be liked, and he seemed to have even less concern over whose toes he might step on, provided that whatever mission had been assigned him was accomplished, the job was done, and he was awarded the highest grades for efficiency, resulting in continued promotion. The Pentagon, the construction of which he directed, was and remains the highest-capacity office building in the world, as well as the largest office building as measured by floor area. Housing some 23,000 military and civilian employees, its corridor space alone totals seventeen and a half miles. Groves built it in just eighteen months.

And with the Pentagon project behind him in 1942, he hoped at last to be sent overseas, into the thick of the war, as a combat engineer. Fighting, after all, was what a soldier did, and it was also the surest route to further promotion. For the past two years, he had been in overall charge of domestic military construction, of which the Pentagon was the crowning project; now this construction was finally on the wane. He had every expectation of shipping out.

Instead, he found himself assigned to a new domestic project, initially as a subordinate to another army engineer, Colonel James C. Marshall. The task was to direct the design and construction of a nuclear-fission weapon, an atomic bomb. This was hardly the same thing as building a building, even one of unprecedented dimensions. In

1942, the idea of a nuclear weapon was still almost entirely theoretical, the airy work of egghead scientists, many of them (Groves understood) refugees from the Nazis, and a lot of them Jews. A hard-nosed, results-oriented engineer, Leslie Groves was at best ambivalent about scientists, especially *theoretical* physicists, whose only tools were pencil and paper. About foreigners and Jews, he was not ambivalent at all. He did not like them. Xenophobia and anti-Semitism were all too typical of the American culture into which Groves had been born and in which he was raised, and, if anything, military life actively nurtured such prejudices. Even as it girded for combat in defense of democracy against the racial hatred promoted by the Nazis and the Japanese, the U.S. Army was at its highest levels largely a closed circle, as restricted along ethnic, racial, and religious lines as the ugliest of country clubs. Groves was every inch a member of the club. Nor were professional, intellectual, personal, and cultural prejudices the only reasons for his lack of enthusiasm about being pressed into service on the new project. Not only would the work delay any assignment overseas, it seemed to him surely doomed to fail. Colonel Marshall was being given a blank check to conjure up an entire weapons system from a mere idea.

Despite his doubts and resentments, Leslie Groves dove into the work, and when it was suggested that the ultra-secret project be cloaked under the name "Laboratory for the Development of Substitute Materials," Groves, objecting that this would only serve to arouse public curiosity rather than deflect it, proposed the code name "Manhattan." It was, he believed, thoroughly innocuous—nothing more than an allusion to the Manhattan Engineer

District, an existing geographical administrative division of the Army Corps of Engineers.

Although it was Groves who gave it the name by which it became known, the Manhattan Project, the race to build an atomic bomb had begun years before he had been drafted into it. Back in 1939, well before the United States entered World War II, a group of American scientists, including recent refugees from European fascist and Nazi regimes, became alarmed by what they were learning about work ongoing in Germany exploring nuclear fission, a process by which the energy of the binding force within the nucleus of the uranium or plutonium atom might be liberated to produce an explosion of unprecedented magnitude. The scientists understood that the work in Germany was being led by no less a figure than Werner Heisenberg, one of the world's leading theoretical physicists. Given Heisenberg's reputation for boundless genius, they believed it highly likely that the work on a fission weapon could very well be carried from theory to reality. Since this particular group of scientists knew only too well what levels of aggression and atrocity Hitler and Mussolini were capable of, they decided to alert the U.S. government and urge that a project to develop fission for military purposes be launched. It would be a race for what might well prove the ultimate weapon.

G. B. Pegram, a Columbia University physicist, brokered a meeting between the eminent physicist Enrico Fermi, a recent refugee from Mussolini's Italy, and the U.S. Department of the Navy in March 1939. In the meantime, Leo Szilard, a Hungarian refugee and physicist, and other scientists prevailed on America's most celebrated and esteemed scientist refugee, Albert Einstein, to endorse a letter to President Franklin D. Roosevelt, advising him of the urgent necessity of beginning work on a military fission project in light of the dangers posed by Germany. The letter was sent on August 2, 1939.

The president read the letter and responded, albeit modestly at first. In February 1940, the miniscule sum of $6,000 was authorized to begin research into the feasibility of building a nuclear fission weapon. The initial investigation was directed by a committee under the chairmanship of L. J. Briggs, head of the National Bureau of Standards. On December 6, 1941—the day before the Japanese attack on Pearl Harbor—direction of the research project was transferred to the Office of Scientific Research and Development, headed by Vannevar Bush, at the time one of the nation's most distinguished and influential scientists. With U.S. entry into the war, the project was injected with a sudden urgency of priority, and the War Department was assigned joint responsibility for it. By the middle of 1942, researchers had concluded that the military application of fission was feasible, but they outlined a monumentally daunting set of required tasks, including the rapid construction of a staggering array of laboratories and mammoth industrial plants—plants that were not only vast, but that were intended to carry out manufacturing processes that, at this point, existed only on the barest of theoretical levels. Classifying this weapons-development project as principally a construction undertaking, the War Department naturally assigned the U.S. Army Corps of Engineers to manage it.

Groves assumed that his association with the Manhattan Project would be mercifully short-lived and would be ended by his assignment overseas. Instead, on September 16, 1942, direction of the entire project was turned over to him. His boss, General Wilhelm Styer, cited reasons for doing this that included Groves's "engineering, administrative and organizing ability; his capacity for work and the fearlessness with which he tackled difficult jobs and the drive and determination with which he pursued them to successful conclusion." Disappointed, Groves swallowed hard and calmly accepted his orders. As if the pressure of actually producing an atomic bomb—out of nothing but theory, at the moment—were not enough, General Thomas M. Robins of the Corps of Engineers remarked to him: "I hate to see you get this assignment, because if you fail in it, it will destroy you. I would be sorry to see that. But it would be still worse if it destroyed the Corps of Engineers. That would really make me sad." Fortunately for himself and the Manhattan Project, Leslie Groves was not a man who needed a pep talk to get things done.

To make the Manhattan Project a success, Groves had to work with a great many people, from politicians to fellow engineers to soldiers to common laborers. But no group was more important than the scientists. It was up to him to assemble the top levels of the scientific team, and he set about to recruit the best and the brightest. Although most of these men were motivated by patriotism—especially strong among the refugees, for whom America was both a hope and a salvation—their entire intellectual and moral orientation was 180 degrees the opposite of Groves's. Groves was a soldier who insisted on adherence to a chain of command and military discipline. Scientists at the level Groves recruited were, in sharp contrast, accustomed to a freedom of thought and imagination bordering on daydreaming. A constant concern of the Manhattan Project was security and secrecy, yet science—especially physics at the cutting edge—lived and breathed on the free exchange of ideas. It was a wholly collaborative endeavor.

On the face of it, there was ample reason for every expectation that Brigadier General (he had been promoted to give him the air of added authority) Leslie R. Groves, capable of driving soldiers and subordinate engineers to do whatever needed to be done, would fail miserably when it came to herding the scientists. Indeed, most of the scientists did regard him with a certain amount of contempt, at least at first. He was pompous, loud, and vain. But he was not stupid, and he was not rigid. He understood that directing scientists was different than commanding troops. He approached them with initial flattery. His message was *you have been chosen because you are the best*. He gave them freedom. *I won't tell you how to do your job*. And he gave them an unambiguous goal. *You must succeed.*

Of all the scientists Groves worked with, the most famous and important was J. Robert Oppenheimer. He was also, quite obviously, the least likely to be personally compatible with Groves. Where Groves verged on rotundity, Oppenheimer was slender to the point of ascetic emaciation. Where Groves bellowed, Oppenheimer was soft spoken. Where Groves was a rightwing military man, Oppenheimer was a leftist intellectual with vaguely communist ties. He was a Jew, and Groves was at least conventionally anti-Semitic; but perhaps worse, Oppenheimer practiced no religion at all and was almost certainly an atheist, whereas Groves was the sincerely believing son of an army chaplain.

There is no doubt that Oppenheimer was a genius. His major at Harvard was chemistry, but he also studied everything from classical Greek, to art, architecture, literature, and then, when he was already a renowned practicing physicist, went on to master Sanskrit so that he could read the Hindu holy scripture, the Bhagavad Gita, in the original. After taking his undergraduate degree, Oppenheimer studied advanced physics in England at the Cavendish Laboratory in Cambridge, working under one of the field's elder statesmen and giants, J. J. Thomson. From there, he went to the University of Göttingen, where he became the protégé of another luminary of modern physics, Max Born. At Göttingen, his circle of friends and colleagues was a who's who of twentieth-century theoretical physics, including Wolfgang Pauli, Paul Dirac, Enrico Fermi, Edward Teller—and Werner Heisenberg. He took his Ph.D. at the tender age of twenty-two. Moving in a world apart from the army engineer, Oppenheimer did share at least one personality trait with Leslie Groves. Although many described his personality as magnetic, others found him hyper-ambitious, all too eager to hijack every intellectual or theoretical discussion, a man driven to the point of sometimes making himself obnoxious to fellow students, colleagues, and even teachers.

Oppenheimer quickly made a name for himself by publishing a number of precocious papers and, in 1927, was eagerly hired by his alma mater, Harvard, to teach mathematical physics. The following year, he moved to Caltech for post-doctoral study, then was appointed to the physics faculty of the University of California, Berkeley, while maintaining a dual appointment at Caltech. Late in

1928, Oppenheimer was invited to the Leiden University, where he delivered lectures on cutting-edge physics in Dutch, despite his almost total unfamiliarity with the language. Back at Berkeley, Oppenheimer became one of the founders of American theoretical physics, yet he was given to profound bouts of melancholy, and while he did important scientific work—including venturing the first theoretical speculations about the existence of black holes in the universe—he did not reach a large scientific audience. His papers, it was said, were extraordinarily difficult, as if he had gone out of his way to make them so. Many of his colleagues began to suspect that his basic research and his theoretical contributions fell short of the potential suggested by his manifest genius. Many suspected that the esoteric nature of some of his writings was intended to cover up basic intellectual shortcomings.

Groves first met Oppenheimer during a tour of the Berkeley laboratories. It is likely that the general knew something of the vague doubts beginning to orbit about the physicist's reputation, but he was thoroughly taken with Oppenheimer from the outset. The scientist known for bewildering his colleagues with abstruse flights of abstraction knew exactly how to speak to Groves. He spoke to him as one engineer to another. Their first conversation was a discussion of what kind of facilities would be required to design and build an atomic bomb. The decisive clarity of Oppenheimer's recommendations impressed Groves and inspired his own final thoughts on how the Manhattan Project laboratories would be structured.

Impressed as he was with Oppenheimer, had Groves listed all the reasons for *not* choosing him to direct the

Manhattan Project laboratories as leader of a vast army of scientists, he could have found plenty. A lifelong sufferer from colitis, Oppenheimer was physically frail and emotionally unstable—at the very least he was high strung. Moreover, he was far from being the most eminent physicist in America, he was politically suspect—a leftist, maybe even an outright communist—his orientation was as far from the military mindset as it is possible to be. Yet as Groves reviewed other possible candidates, Oppenheimer always stubbornly rose to the top. Groves understood that he needed more than a brilliant theoretician. He needed a scientist leader. Leo Szilard was easily a more original thinker than Oppenheimer, but he was also so overbearing that people tended to shun him and shut him out. Harold Urey, a distinguished Nobel laureate, was highly esteemed, but also something of a shrinking violet, unwilling to assert himself in an administrative role. There were others, but Groves saw in Oppenheimer precisely the spark he needed to accomplish the mission of transforming mere theory into a working weapon. Others, including a number of prominent scientists, protested that Oppenheimer had never run a laboratory and had neither experience with nor interest in administration. Urey, Arthur Compton, and Ernest Lawrence, all acknowledged giants of American physics, all held Nobel Prizes. Oppenheimer did not. Only a Nobel, some scientists cautioned, carried with it the kind of prestige necessary to get any number of scientists in line behind a leader. But Groves countered that there was something naturally inspiring about J. Robert Oppenheimer. He had what military men call "command presence." Moreover, he was polished, capable of exerting great personal charm, and was willing to support the ideas of others. Whatever his shortcomings might be as a truly original theoretician, he was capable of understanding the most novel and complex problems with dazzling speed, thoroughness, and crystal clarity. Nor was he a loner. He listened carefully. He was tolerant of a wide array of opposing ideas. He had the gift of synthesizing differing points of view into a productive approach to a given problem.

In the end, Groves did not look back. Oppenheimer was the man he wanted to direct the scientific work of the Manhattan Project. Oppenheimer would be his partner, the scientific chief on whose success or failure would depend the success or failure of the atomic bomb project—and the future of Leslie R. Groves. As for Oppenheimer himself, he had no illusions as to why he had been chosen. The general, he later told a journalist, "had a fatal weakness for good men." It was as if J. Robert Oppenheimer had somehow felt himself destined to do this extraordinary work and, without any false modesty, acknowledged in Leslie R. Groves the very man who recognized his destiny.

Oppenheimer accepted the challenge, but, unlike the general, he did look back. When a test bomb was detonated at 5:30 A.M. on July 16, 1945, at a remote location near Alamogordo, New Mexico, Oppenheimer later recalled that the words of the Bhagavad Gita had come into his mind:

> If the radiance of a thousand suns
> Were to burst into the sky
> That would be like
> The splendor of the Mighty One . . .
> I am become Death, the shatterer of worlds.

Perhaps those words really did occur to him then and there. Like many of the others who had worked on the Manhattan Project, Oppenheimer was tortured by conscience afterward and to the end of his life. At the time of the explosion, however, the scientist's brother, Frank (also present at the test), reported that the only words to fall from Oppenheimer's lips were "It worked."

J. Robert Oppenheimer was a complicated man, in fragile health and emotionally volatile. All during his work on the bomb, he must have shown signs of stress. Were these due to doubts of conscience? Or to fear that "the gadget" (as the scientists called their project) wouldn't work? We don't know. We do know, however, that Groves, whatever doubts he may have had, invariably acted the role of the effective military commander. He never revealed anything to "his men"—the project scientists—other than complete confidence in the successful completion of the bomb, their mission. At times, we know, this deliberately superficial attitude grated on Oppenheimer, but it also carried him along, despite whatever emotional baggage he himself carried. A brilliant administrator, Groves was also a leader who conceived his mission not so much as summarily ordering Oppenheimer and the other scientists around—they would not have responded well to that—but as transforming himself into a kind of ultra-reliable vehicle to keep them all moving forward.

∽✆∾

FOR ALL HIS BLUSTER, for all his single-minded focus on the mission, Leslie Groves had a keen intuition of what would keep the likes of J. Robert Oppenheimer going. True, he inhabited a theoretical, emotional, religious, and political realm worlds apart from the general. Yet Groves saw that, at some deep level, both he and Oppenheimer shared a relentless ambition. He also recognized that, just as he himself had been thwarted in his desire for the highest glory and fulfillment of a professional soldier—field command in combat—Oppenheimer had never quite fully realized his own promise as a theoretical physicist. If both shared ambition, they also had in common an essential, deep-seated frustration, a certain generalized disappointment in their lives and careers. Having viewed the Manhattan Project as yet another professional disappointment, Groves had rapidly come to believe that it *could* be made to work. This half-hearted hope metamorphosed into an absolute conviction that it *must* be made to work—and not just to beat the Germans to the bomb and to end the war, but to elevate his own career above that of any mere field commander. Now, unbridled ambition can be an ugly and destructive force, unless a person possessed the leadership gift of attracting others into the orbit of one's own ambition. And that is precisely what Leslie Groves was able to do with J. Robert Oppenheimer.

TAKEAWAY

AS DIFFERENT AS THEY WERE, Groves never really had to woo the scientist. From their very first meeting, this apparently unlikely pair hit it off and did so on a level that went far beyond the merely personal. They seemed to recognize in one another—instantly—the components of mind, will, imagination, and personality each needed to complete himself. Individually, neither man was capable of leading the building of the atomic bomb. Together, they possessed the qualities necessary to do just that. And whatever else the bomb would mean—victory, peace, mass death, technological atrocity, a world forever afterward shadowed by the specter of Armageddon—it meant to Groves and Oppenheimer an achievement indisputable. Thanks to each other, the world, whatever might be left of it, would remember their names forever.

CHAPTER 9

The Tito Factor

The Story of a Pragmatic Marxist

Previous page: *Josep Broz Tito (far right) with Yugoslav partisans, ca. 1943.*

The Tito Factor

FOR MOST OF ITS HISTORY, the Balkans consisted of such fragmented and jarring states, provinces, possessions, and principalities that, in the early twentieth century, the word *balkanize* was coined to describe any situation in which a region or territory had been carved up into small, hostile pieces. Famously, after playing Europe in the late 1800s as if it were a nineteenth-century prototype of RISK, Germany's Otto von Bismarck contemplated his handiwork—an apparently stable continent anchored by a triumphant new German empire—and, in an unsourced but universally repeated pronouncement, declared that the next major war would begin over "some damn fool thing in the Balkans." The region was—and, in the 1990s, became again—a synonym for violent disorder and political volatility.

When Josip Broz—he would, years later, enter the world stage under the pseudonym of Tito—was born in 1892, his village of Kumrovec was part of Croatia, which belonged to the Austro-Hungarian Empire, along with Slovenia, Bosnia and Herzegovina, Vojvodina, and Transylvania. At this time the neighboring Balkan territory of northern Bulgaria was a nominally sovereign principality that was actually a vassal to the Ottoman Empire, and southern Bulgaria was an Ottoman province, as were Albania, Kosovo, Macedonia, Novi Pazar (between Serbia and Montenegro), and northern Greece. Moldava belonged to Russia. On the Balkan peninsula, only Serbia, Montenegro, Romania, and southern Greece were truly independent, sovereign states. All of these political divisions were ultimately arbitrary. The Balkans was a crazy quilt of nationalities and ethnic and religious groups, almost tribal in nature, concentrating in a small area a multiplicity of languages and dialects.

Born on a Kumrovec farm, Broz drifted through a succession of factory jobs in a series of Balkan cities and towns, organized labor movements, became a communist, endured multiple arrests and imprisonments, fought two world wars, and, as Tito, forged out of the "balkanized" Balkans a multiethnic, multireligious, multinational nation—relatively prosperous, beholden neither to the Soviet-dominated East nor to the Anglo-American-dominated West, yet reasonably friendly with both, and, at least as long as Tito lived, almost miraculously unified. It was an achievement built in part on luck, on Tito's personal courage and charisma, on the judicious use of force as well as outright oppression, but, most of all, on exquisitely engineered and managed strategic alliances, in which Broz—as Tito—combined political ideology with opportunistic pragmatism.

By the age of eight, Josip Broz was doing farm work while attending school, leaving the classroom four years later to become a full-time cowherd. In 1907, when he was fifteen, Broz went off to the town of Sisak, where he found work as a waiter. Three years later, it was on to the large cities of Zagreb, Ljubljana, and Trieste for factory work. By 1912, Broz was living near Vienna with his brother, was becoming increasingly active in the workers' movement, and was drifting closer to socialism and communism when, in 1913, at the age of twenty-one, he was drafted into the Austro-Hungarian army.

For the young Croat, this meant serving in what he later recalled in an interview as "an army of oppression, which not only held my people in subjection, but served as an instrument to enslave other nations." Moreover, "it was an old-fashioned and unintelligent army. It operated by rule and formula and instead of teaching men how to fight taught them how to drill." Even so, Broz discovered a taste for military life and proved to be a very good soldier, quickly rising to the rank of staff sergeant, becoming an adept skier, and a champion fencer. Indeed, Broz managed to learn even from the stupidity of the Hapsburg army. He learned to recognize all of the weaknesses of conventional, hidebound, outmoded military institutions. He learned how *not* to lead men in combat. When the Great War—World War I—broke out at the end of July 1914, he was not yet enough of a communist to obey Lenin's international call to his followers not to fight. On the contrary, Broz eagerly accepted an assignment commanding an elite reconnaissance platoon, which gave him a very different experience from the vast majority of soldiers in the war. On most fronts and for most troops, the Great War was a mindless slaughter defined by static lines of opposed trenches. For Broz and his platoon, it was a series of daring adventures behind enemy lines. He had already learned the ways in which an army could be stupid. Now he learned how to make allies of stealth, surprise, and small-unit agility. He learned the art of infiltration. He learned the aggressive tactics of hit and run. He learned how to fight a guerrilla war.

Needless to say, it was very dangerous work, and on Easter morning 1915, the regiment to which he was attached was overrun by the Czar's Circassian mounted lancers on the banks of the River Dniester. Broz was literally transfixed—run through the back by a Circassian lance—and fell to the ground unconscious. Just as one of the cavalrymen was about to finish him off, Russian infantry followed the wave of lancers and ordered a halt to the slaughter. Broz was duly collected as a prisoner of war and taken far to the rear, to the Siberian village of Shvishk on the River Volga, where he was lodged in an Orthodox monastery and nursed back to health, surviving infection, pneumonia, and typhus. As Neil Barnett relates in his biography, *Tito,* Broz passed the tedious hours of his recovery learning Russian and reading Russian literature, but when he was invited to join the Russian army, he refused—as a Croat, he identified neither with the Austro-Hungarian Empire nor with that of the empire of the Russians—and was sent to a POW camp even farther east.

Camp life was predictably brutal, but Broz never allowed himself to be a victim. He assumed command of some four hundred inmates, who were assigned to work on Russian rail lines, but when he proved too defiant for his overseers, he was beaten by Cossack guards and thrown into a cell. While languishing one day, he heard cries of "Down with the Tsar," and was quickly freed—along with the other POWs—by local workers, who had learned of the downfall of Nicholas II in the revolution.

Broz did not long enjoy his freedom. The pro-Western provisional republican government of Alexander Kerensky threw as many Bolsheviks as they could lay their hands on back into prison. Assigned again to railroad work, Broz escaped and made his way to St. Petersburg, where he was caught up in a violent demonstration against the provisional government. With Kerensky's authorities closing in, he attempted to flee to Finland, was arrested, confined, then packed off to Siberia, but—yet again—managed to escape and, this time, made his way to a Bolshevik strong-hold in Omsk. For the next two years, he fought in, lived through, and survived the bitter civil war that followed the Bolshevik Revolution, and in 1920 joined the Russian Communist Party, returning to Croatia the next year to bring the people's revolution to his homeland.

The Treaty of Versailles that ended World War I dismantled the Austro-Hungarian Empire only to lump together Croatia and many of the other Balkan states and former provinces into the Kingdom of Serbs, Croats and Slovenes—essentially putting everyone, regardless of ethnicity or national affiliation, under the thumb of the Serbian King Aleksander, whose government was at least as corrupt, inefficient, oppressive, and unwelcome as that of the Hapsburgs. Broz aggressively worked toward revolu-tion and proved a brilliant and charismatic labor agitator and organizer. Jailed at various times, he took advantage of each of his incarcerations to radicalize his fellow inmates. Although he was a proud Croatian, Broz was an even more dedicated Communist, and he subordinated his nation-alist impulses to the will of Moscow. The Soviet Communist leaders recognized him as both ambitious and obedient, so that he rose rapidly within the Party. Arrested in 1928, he readily admitted to membership in the illegal Communist Party of Yugoslavia (so the party called itself, even though the Kingdom of Serbs, Croats, and Slovenes would not be officially reconstituted as Yugoslavia until 1929) and impressed everyone—the public, his defense attorneys, and even the prosecution—with his charisma. One rightwing reporter admiringly noted that "his face makes one think of steel." Broz was sentenced to five years' hard labor.

As usual, he made the best of his time in prison, establishing productive contact with fellow communists and managing to organize a communist group in jail. "It was," he said later, "just like being in a university." Moreover, it kept him safely isolated from the police terror and rightwing vigilantism ongoing in Yugoslavia, which included the assassination or execution of many radicals like himself. By the time he was released in March 1934, Yugoslavia was torn between the communists and the newly emerged fascist party, the Ustaše, which was supported in part by Germany's Hitler and Italy's Mussolini. Broz made his way to Zagreb, where he found the Communist Party, in contrast to the rising fascists, largely shorn of leadership, the top men having either fallen victim to political violence or fled into exile. Thus Broz was catapulted to a leadership position by default. The vacuum had to be filled. And it was now that he took his pseudonym, Tito. Although he himself later claimed that the choice of the name was quite arbitrary—"it occurred to me at the moment"—others have said that it came from his clipped, decisive, and laconic style of issuing orders. He would merely point to a man and quietly say, "You, this"—in Serbo-Croat, "Ti, to."

Whatever their origin, the choice of these two simple syllables served to nurture and promote what was quickly becoming a legendary status among Yugoslav Communists. On all sides, both within the Party and without, "Tito" was credited—or blamed—for virtually every labor strike and demonstration that broke out. By 1937, he was officially secretary-general—in effect, leader—of the Yugoslav Communist Party, and he wasted no time in filling the topmost Party posts with his most trusted comrades. From the beginning of his real power, Tito exerted command and control in a most personal manner.

As he rose in the Party, Tito came to realize that the fascists and the capitalists were not his only enemies. Joseph Stalin, absolute dictator of the Soviet Union and high priest of international communism, spent a good part of the 1930s purging the Communist Party. Unpredictable and ruthless, the only apparent constant in his personality was a driving need to possess and control all power absolutely. Rise too high in the Party or loom too brightly in the eyes of the people, and Comrade Stalin would not think twice before mowing off your head.

When Stalin stunned the world by concluding a nonaggression pact with Adolf Hitler on August 24, 1939, signifying a virtual alliance between communism and fascism, Tito did his best to exercise self-restraint; speaking of himself and his followers, he said that we "accepted the pact like disciplined communists, considering it necessary for the security of the Soviet Union." At the same time, however, he declared that the Hitler-Stalin Pact "did not for a moment weaken our vigilance in preparing for the defense of our homeland in the event of attack" by Germany. Tito had learned an important secret of the true meaning of "alliance" within the Communist Party. It was this: he needed Stalin, so he obeyed Stalin, but he never trusted Stalin. And he was preparing to separate himself—as well as his Yugoslav Communists—from Stalin. In short, Tito had learned the art of holding simultaneously in mind two opposing positions, giving each equal weight, and acting on one or the other, variously, as events indicated.

Days after concluding the pact with Stalin, Hitler started World War II by invading Poland on September 1, 1939. On March 25, 1941, Prince Paul, regent to Yugoslavia's underage crown prince, Peter, caved in to pressure from Hitler and joined the German-Italian-Japanese "Axis." On the streets of all Yugoslav cities, the result of this was a popular riot, which was followed by a military coup that ousted Paul, proclaimed the crown prince king, and installed the leader of the coup, air force general Dušan Simović, as acting prime minister. Yet, just days after he assumed office, Simović, also folded, declaring that the new government would adhere to the Axis Pact after all. If Simović had thought to placate Adolf Hitler, however, he was tragically mistaken. On April 6, the Führer ordered the commencement of "Operation Punishment," an invasion of Yugoslavia led off by massive air raids on Belgrade. Yugoslavia fell quickly and was greedily carved up among Germany, Italy, and the fascist Ustaše. As for Tito, he submerged himself, temporarily assumed a new identity, as the engineer Slavko Babic , and remained underground in Zagreb and then Belgrade, apparently pondering how to respond to invasion by a country that was, by virtue of the Hitler-Stalin Pact, actually allied to the Soviet Union.

He did not wait long. When Stalin ejected the Yugoslav ambassador from Moscow in April—arguing that, because Yugoslavia had ceased to exist, there was no need for the presence of an ambassador—Tito called a meeting of the Central Committee of the Yugoslav Communist Party and ordered the commencement of national resistance to the invaders, Stalin or no Stalin. As a practical matter, however, there was little that could be done immediately, especially without support from the USSR. This situation also soon changed. On June 22, 1941, Adolf Hitler unilaterally abrogated his pact with Stalin by invading the Soviet Union. The Comintern—Moscow-based international Communist Party headquarters—reached out to Tito, asking not that he work to liberate Yugoslavia so much as that he "start a partisan war in the enemy's rear." Tito understood that, whatever the war was called—a war of national liberation or a war in aid of the Soviet Union—it came to the same thing: a fight to disrupt the German offensive. Rather than risk diluting the newly urgent alliance between his partisans and the Soviet Union, therefore, he put his orders in terms designed to appeal directly to Stalin: "The war of the Soviet Union," he told his followers, "is your war, because the Soviet Union is fighting your enemies." Willing to oppose Stalin when Stalin abandoned his country, Tito embraced him patriotically when Yugoslavia suddenly loomed as a valuable Soviet ally. There was nothing personal about it. It was a matter of putting just the right spin on an expedient political alliance.

Tito led his partisans in relentless guerrilla warfare against the Germans. His strategy was always to remain on the offensive, to hit and run, and never to try to hold territory. His tactics were stealth, surprise, and mobility. Ostensibly, another group—officially known as the Yugoslav Home Army, but better known as the Četniks—was also fighting the resistance against the invaders. The Četniks, however, were royalist conservatives, and their "resistance" was often so cautious as to verge on outright collaboration with the Germans. Tito made an uneasy alliance with the Četniks, only to find them frequently attacking his partisans. Worse, for a good part of the war, the Četniks were receiving support from the British and Americans, whereas the partisans were almost entirely neglected. Try as he might to work with the Četniks as an ally, Tito realized that resistance to the Germans was part of what had become a civil war between the communist partisans and the rightist, royalist Četniks. The Četniks sometimes treated the partisans as allies, sometimes as an enemy, and this was true of their approach to the Germans as well.

But this was not the only problem Tito faced. Although he had faithfully led his partisans in operations specifically ordered by Moscow, the Soviet Union had not sent a single weapon or bullet to Tito's forces, and Tito's Soviet contacts repeatedly ignored his requests for aid. This unresponsiveness was not due to a shortage of supplies or even to Stalin's ambivalence about Tito, whose popular magnetism he certainly feared. More than anything, it was the product of Stalin's own difficult position with regard to his Western Allies, the United States and Great Britain. Stalin did not want to give these powerful forces the impression that the Comintern was arming Eastern European countries for the purposes of spreading the communist revolution after the war. Indeed, he was so afraid of alienating Roosevelt and Churchill that, in 1943, at the very height of the war, he disbanded the Comintern, which had been the chief organ of international communism since the days of Lenin. Whatever else Stalin was, he was the supreme pragmatist, and if keeping his strange

146

Western bedfellows comfortable required setting aside the mission of disseminating communism worldwide, so be it.

By 1943, then, Tito had moral but no material support from Moscow, and he had a wholly dysfunctional alliance with the Četniks, who, however, received virtually all of the support the Western Allies were funneling into Yugoslavia. Fortunately, at precisely this moment—the point at which the partisan position was beginning to look untenable—British intelligence began revealing to Churchill that the Četniks were at best overcautious and at worst collaborationist, whereas the partisans had been grossly underestimated and were at all times both aggressive and highly effective. The British prime minister dispatched a special military mission under Captain Bill Deakin to investigate. Tito reached out to him, and the man whose face had once been described as steel greeted Deakin like a comrade-at-arms. Tito's warmth and openness charmed Deakin, and the Croat's leadership of the partisans impressed him. Quite won over, Deakin sent glowing reports to Churchill, who responded by dispatching Brigadier General Fitzroy Maclean to Tito's headquarters to create a close military liaison and alliance.

Having secured at long last the support of the British, and following repeated military successes against the Germans, Tito looked at the wider picture. Everywhere the Germans were now in retreat. He therefore convened a meeting of communist delegates from all over Yugoslavia, who approved the immediate creation of a provisional government, with Tito as both prime minister and minister of defense. In addition, he took the military title of "Marshal of Yugoslavia." Because Stalin wanted to keep his Western alliance well lubricated, he took the unusual step of encouraging Tito to create a singularly liberal government, in which the rights of self-determination and private property were guaranteed, and no plans were announced to abolish the monarchy. Thinking it would please the British, Stalin, however, wanted Tito to go further by opening a direct diplomatic line between the provisional government and the royal Yugoslav government in exile. Tito refused, dispatching a communiqué to Moscow announcing that his followers—the members of the provisional government of Yugoslavia—had "empowered" him to declare that "we acknowledge neither the Yugoslav Government nor the King abroad." The reason was that the king and his government-in-exile had supported collaborationists in Yugoslavia and had thus committed "treason to the peoples of Yugoslavia." Moreover, the king and his government would not be allowed to return to Yugoslavia "because this would mean civil war"—as if civil war were not already ongoing.

Not one accustomed to defiance, Stalin was furious. But then he looked to the West and, seeing that Tito's declaration actually sat well with the British and Americans—who were all for "democratic" self-determination—Stalin swallowed hard and bowed to Marshal Tito.

When Germany surrendered on May 7–8, 1945, not only did Tito stand as leader of Yugoslavia but also he had the unique distinction among all Eastern European political figures of having led the liberation of his own country. His partisans had driven the Germans out, whereas, in the other countries bordering the Soviet Union, the Red Army had done the job and now occupied the lands it had "liberated." For this reason, Tito believed he had earned autonomy and independence from Stalin. Before the war ended, Churchill and Stalin had agreed on the roles the Western Allies and the Soviet Union would play in the postwar Balkans. In exchange for a 50/50 split of West-East influence in Yugoslavia, Churchill conceded the Soviets a 90 percent influence stake in Romania and a 75 percent stake in Bulgaria. Apportioning a 50/50 influence in Yugoslavia between Britain and the Soviets required securing Tito's cooperation, including his submission to Stalin and his agreement to tone down the hardcore Marxist rhetoric he had long favored. But the Red Army did not occupy Yugoslavia, and Tito therefore saw no reason for slavish obedience to Stalin. He did not, therefore, countenance the agreement with Churchill.

If Tito refused to yield to Stalin, so he declined to bow to Churchill as well. As the war was winding down, Tito had requested a meeting with Stalin to discuss final actions and troop movements across Yugoslav territory. Stalin agreed to the meeting, but requested that Tito keep it secret from the British, so as not to alarm or offend them. Tito did no such thing, and when the chief of the British Mission complained about his conferring with Stalin without having first informed Prime Minister Churchill, Tito calmly replied, "Only recently Mr. Churchill went to Quebec to see President Roosevelt and I only heard of this visit after he returned. And I was not angry."

The remark was vintage Tito. It was firm, yet disarming in its charm—and unassailable in its logic. Tito intended to make alliances, but they would begin and end precisely in accordance with what he saw as the self-interest of

Yugoslavia. For the most part, the West responded amicably to this approach, and, while East-West relations following World War II were largely defined by the smoldering hostility of the Cold War, Western relations with Tito's Yugoslavia included extensive trade and considerable tourism. Stalin repeatedly tried to end Tito's rule over Yugoslavia in the postwar years, through a punishing economic blockade and through naked attempts to bring about a coup d'etat. He failed. He also failed in his efforts to have Tito killed. After Stalin's death in 1953, a letter from Tito was found in a writing table in Stalin's dacha (summer house):

> Stalin: Stop sending people to kill me. We've already captured five of them, one of them with a bomb and another with a rifle. If you don't stop sending killers, I'll send one to Moscow and I won't have to send a second.

One of Stalin's biographers, Robert Service, remarked of this letter that it was an instance of "one gangster" writing to another. If Stalin was at bottom a "gangster," so, clearly, Tito showed that he was comfortable in that role as well. Tito insisted on being treated as an equal—and on terms of equality he himself defined.

And that in itself was intolerable to Joseph Stalin. Tito represented a threat to his power. Thanks to Tito's military and political leadership during the war, Yugoslavia was neither occupied by nor beholden to the Soviet Union. It had liberated itself. Tito was not the typical puppet of the Soviet satellites. If anything, he was a leader akin to Stalin himself—more polished, to be sure, more self-controlled, yet committed to holding absolute power and willing to exercise brute force and terror when he felt they were called for. But he was never dogmatic about it. As Barnett observes, he once explained that the cause of the conflict between Yugoslavia and the USSR was "simple." The Soviet Union "had reached stagnation point in its development. The trend towards State capitalism was disenfranchising the workers" and the Soviet Union had "become an enormous terror state." As Tito saw it, Stalin had betrayed the ultimate goal of a Marxist revolution, which was the "disappearance" of the state. What Tito called "State capitalism"—an economy and system of government in which everyone was effectively enslaved to a centralized state—was no more Marxist than the most capitalist of capitalist systems. In fact, Tito came to believe, capitalism was closer to the Marxist ideal of the decentralized, disappearing state than Stalinism was. Not that he himself wanted to disappear, but he did believe that Yugoslavia could benefit from cordial relations with both the West and the East, and he concluded that the best way to maintain that cordiality with both poles of the Cold War era was to maintain a scrupulously independent course, always offering something to both sides—well short of actual allegiance to either.

I N THE END, THE LONG REIGN OF TITO of Yugoslavia was remarkable. His nation remained a communist country, but it prospered almost as if it were fully a part of the Western capitalist sphere.

TAKEAWAY

TITO WAS, TO BE SURE, a dictator, albeit, compared to Stalin and his ilk, relatively benign. Yet his rule was marked by one great flaw. It was a government of a man, not of laws. Yugoslavia was held together by a cult of personality dedicated to Marshal Tito. For all his successes, he failed to provide for a viable successor, let alone a form of government that would maintain the unity of Yugoslavia after he was no longer in power. Shortly after his death in 1980, on May 4, three days short of his eighty-eighth birthday, Yugoslavia began to fall apart, returning to the fractured, volatile, violent entity into which Josip Broz had been born nearly nine full decades earlier. Absent the powerful presence of Tito, the brilliantly managed alliance with two worlds—the communist and the capitalist—ceased to have any meaning at all.

CHAPTER 10

41 and 42

*The Partnership of
George H. W. Bush and Bill Clinton*

∽∾

Previous page: *Former U.S. presidents George H. W. Bush and Bill Clinton arrive at Malé international airport in the Maldives, February 21, 2005.*

41 and 42

JUST BEFORE ONE O'CLOCK IN THE MORNING on December 26, 2004, the earth beneath the Indian Ocean off the west coast of Sumatra, Indonesia, exploded in the second most powerful quake ever recorded on a seismograph. Measuring between 9.1 and 9.3 on the 10-point Richter scale, it lasted in places for an incredible ten minutes—the longest earthquake ever observed anywhere. All of the planet "felt" it, vibrating as much as a half inch, and sympathetic tremors were touched off in various vulnerable areas—even as far away as Alaska. But it was what happened along virtually all of the coastal areas of the Indian Ocean that brought devastation on an unprecedented scale. Tsunamis slammed into the coasts of eleven nations, bringing towering walls of ocean as high as a hundred feet advancing at high speed across beaches, drowning entire villages and towns in unimaginable volumes of water, and killing more than a quarter of a million people—most of them in Indonesia, Sri Lanka, India, and Thailand.

On January 3, 2005, President George W. Bush recruited his father, George H. W. Bush, to partner with none other than the man who had defeated him for reelection in 1992, Bill Clinton. Former first lady Barbara Bush, George H. W.'s wife and George W.'s mother, dubbed the team of the former forty-first and forty-second presidents the "Odd Couple," an allusion to the 1965 Neil Simon Broadway hit comedy on which an enormously popular television sitcom was based in the 1970s and early 1980s. Simon's premise was simple. He told the story of two grown men with fundamentally opposite personalities, interests, and values who are compelled by circumstance to become unwilling roommates, in the process forging a comical but warm bond. It would be inaccurate to call the senior Bush and Bill Clinton political enemies—they were never outright enemies—but they were surely rivals, the victory of one requiring the defeat of the other. They had been the standard bearers of opposing political parties in a time of unprecedented and increasingly bitter divisiveness in American politics, which were marked not by mere differences in policy, but by a seemingly unbridgeable gulf over issues of moral, religious, and cultural values.

Barbara Bush was right. On the face of it, they were the Odd Couple, outwardly ill-suited to collaborate on anything of any importance. Yet when it came to heading up fundraising efforts for tsunami relief, neither man hesitated. Clinton later explained that he had been contemplating starting his own fundraising effort when he received the call from the White House asking him to join forces with the forty-first president. Clearly, Clinton did not hesitate, and both he and the senior Bush were quick to appreciate that, working together, they could raise far more money than they could working separately. This was not just because each former president possessed his own unique list of wealthy and influential potential donors, but because the symbolism of two political rivals—representatives of deeply differing values—working together would be virtually impossible to resist. The two men acknowledged that the nation was divided, but recognized that all Americans had a powerful need to unite on something worthwhile. Tsunami relief readily transcended partisan politics and provided a reason for people of every political stripe to come together. The partnership of past rivals for the highest office in the land was the perfect emblem of a united effort in which everyone could participate and feel good about doing so. Thus, the tsunami offered a unique situation in which opponents made for the perfect allies—precisely because of their differences.

Those differences ran deep, deeper than mere party affiliation. George Herbert Walker Bush and William Jefferson Clinton were both Americans, to be sure, but they came from very different worlds. Bush was the scion of privilege and old money, having been raised in Greenwich, Connecticut, the son of a Wall Street banker who was elected to the United States Senate in 1952, serving until 1963. At Yale, Bush was enrolled in the legendary Skull and Bones, the secret society whose membership constituted a significant fraction of the nation's inner circle of financial and political influence. Whereas Bush had been born and bred into the Establishment, Clinton started life far from even the outermost fringes of the American dream. He was born in the town of Hope, Arkansas, a name well-nigh allegorical as a description of what would be the arc of the young man's life. His father, William Jefferson Blythe Jr., a traveling salesman heavily freighted with all the pop cultural baggage that profession entails, was in every sense a wandering man. His son never knew him, because he was killed in an automobile accident some three months before his birth. Blythe's widow, Virginia Dell Cassidy, was remarried in 1950 to Roger Clinton, a partner in a car dealership. William Jefferson Blythe III, known as Billy, did not formally adopt the name Clinton until he was fourteen.

Whereas Bush enjoyed a close relationship with his prosperous and highly regarded father, Clinton did his best to cope with his stepfather's alcohol-fueled abuse of his mother. Young Clinton found an escape in music, which he loved. He played the saxophone, and even thought about becoming a professional musician. But at Hot Springs High School—a milieu very different from Greenwich Country Day School and Phillips Academy where Bush had received his precollege education—he became enthusiastically involved in student government and, as he related in his autobiography, sometime in his sixteenth year decided he "wanted to be in public life as an elected official." Whereas Bush had been born into public service at a high level, Clinton found his own way in and up. In 1963, as a Boys Nation "senator," he met President John F. Kennedy at the White House. That same year, he was mesmerized by the "I Have a Dream" speech delivered from the steps of the Lincoln Memorial by Martin Luther King Jr. On scholarship, Clinton attended the Edmund A. Walsh School of Foreign Service at Georgetown University, before being awarded a Rhodes Scholarship to University College, Oxford, where he continued his studies in government. Whereas Bush, more than two decades Clinton's senior, had been a naval aviator in World War II—twice shot down and decorated with the Distinguished Flying Cross—Clinton participated in anti-Vietnam War protests while studying abroad. Like Bush, he did enroll at Yale, but in the law school rather than as an undergraduate. Clinton earned his law degree in 1973.

Both men served their county, albeit along sharply diverging paths. After his World War II service and graduation from Yale in 1948, George H. W. Bush went into the oil exploration business, working for a subsidiary of Brown Brothers Harriman, the financial house of which his father was a director. Then he partnered in another oil enterprise before running for the Senate in 1964. Defeated by the incumbent Democrat, Ralph Yarborough, Bush endured his opponent's accusations that he was an ultra-conservative "tool of the eastern kingmakers." Bush came back two years later, however, and this time won a seat in the House of Representatives. He next ran for the Senate, again without success, and in 1971 was appointed ambassador to the United Nations by President Richard Nixon. After leaving that post in 1973, Bush chaired the Republican National Committee and became Nixon's staunch defender during the Watergate scandal. President Gerald R. Ford appointed him chief of the U.S. Liaison Office in the People's Republic of China—a position that effectively made him ambassador to China in all but name—then in 1976 recalled him to serve as director of the Central Intelligence Agency (CIA). After Democrat Jimmy Carter entered the White House in 1977, Bush returned to the private sector as chairman of the First International Bank in Houston. Three years later, he sought the Republican presidential nomination in 1980, losing it to Ronald Reagan, who tapped him as his running mate. George H. W. Bush served as vice president of the United States through both of Reagan's terms, then went on to defeat Democrat Michael Dukakis in 1988 and become the nation's forty-first president.

After he earned his law degree, Clinton was hired by the University of Arkansas as a law professor. He made an unsuccessful bid for the House of Representatives in 1974, but two years later won election as attorney general of Arkansas. In 1978, he ran successfully in the state's gubernatorial election, becoming, at thirty-two, the youngest governor in the nation. Defeated for reelection two years later, he regained the office in 1982 and served for ten more years, emerging as one of the vanguard of the so-called "New Democrats," a centrist movement within the party that espoused such Republicanesque goals as welfare reform and the shrinking of government. Although many traditional Democrats objected to what they regarded as a betrayal of the party's liberal values, Clinton's multiple terms as Arkansas governor had done much to stimulate growth in the economy and in jobs. Incentives he introduced also vastly improved what had been a dismal state record in public education. By 1992, Bill Clinton had achieved a sufficiently prominent national profile to win the Democratic nomination for president. Running on a platform that stressed economic reform during a period of recession, Clinton defeated incumbent George H. W. Bush by a substantial margin.

In the wake of the 2004 tsunami, Bush and Clinton proved to be phenomenally effective fundraisers, drumming up a record-breaking billion dollars in a remarkably brief period. Both men had a keen understanding of the meaning of their alliance. As Bush told NBC reporter Jamie Gangel in a May 6, 2005, interview, "We had the satisfaction of knowing that we were doing something bigger than ourselves." In the same interview, Clinton noted that seeing the children in the devastated region—how they "were left behind," their parents dead—

affected him deeply. Even before he finished his sentence about the children, he interrupted himself to observe, "I know George felt this way." It was a casual remark that demonstrated how closely in tune the feelings of the two allies were. They responded to the same basic human needs, and they did so in a way, Bush observed, that sent "a signal around the world [that] you can be political opponents and still work together for something more important than your own political future."

In the alliance of two former rivals, neither of whom had renounced his allegiance to his own political party and its values, was an undeniable nobility as well as extraordinary effectiveness. These qualities were reiterated in September 2005, when Bush and Clinton joined forces again, this time to raise money for Hurricane Katrina relief, addressing the huge gap between the faltering federal and state efforts to help victims and the victims' vast and pressing need. Even as he reactivated his partnership with Clinton, the senior Bush must have known that he would be asked hard questions about the torrent of criticism leveled at his son, George W. Bush, on account of the government's many stunning failures in responding to Katrina. Referring to the criticism, the senior Bush remarked on September 6, "The president can take it," and with that, focused instead on his own work with Clinton. For his part, Clinton studiously avoided criticizing the current Bush administration or anyone else at any level of government. He, too, kept the focus on fundraising rather than politics. By June 2006, when it was announced that Bush and Clinton were to be awarded that year's Liberty Medal at the National

Constitution Center in Philadelphia, they had together raised more than $130 million for Katrina relief.

Not everyone was persuaded that the Bush-Clinton alliance was entirely selfless. NBC's Jamie Gangel raised the issue in her May 6, 2005, interview with the two men. "The word is," she said, "you genuinely like each other," but, she continued, "you both know that the chattering class in Washington is convinced that there must be some angle, some political motivation." Turning to Bill Clinton, Gangel alluded to "speculation [that] this is about appealing to those red state voters if your wife should decide to run for president," and then directing herself to George H. W. Bush, she continued: "President Bush, maybe so that in a polarizing time, it would help your son."

Both men denied any ulterior motives, but Clinton did provide a frank analysis of just why they could afford to abandon such motives in this alliance: "You know, maybe it's easier for us because we've slaked our ambition. We got to do our lives. We got to live the lives we dreamed of."

REMARKABLE AS THE PARTNERSHIP OF PRESIDENTS forty-one and forty-two was, the altruism on which it was based doubtless had its limit—or, more precisely, the alliance was made possible by the existence of a firmly established foundation of goals already attained, achievements already realized, ambitions already "slaked." Though well short of saintly in its rise above partisan politics-as-usual, the Bush-Clinton alliance was extraordinary and extraordinarily effective.

TAKEAWAY

ONE OF THE GREAT PLEASURES of an all-absorbing, highly challenging game like RISK is that the fiercest competitors often develop intense feelings of mutual admiration. Rivals can either choose to be bitter personal enemies, or they can learn to respect one another's strengths and, from this position of respect, convert rivalry into an effective alliance. The philosopher Hegel believed that the greatest intellectual progress was made by the action of "thesis" and "antithesis"—fundamental opposites. Something analogous can happen when hard-tested rivals resolve to join forces.

BIBLIOGRAPHY

Introduction

Axelrod, Alan. *Everything I Know about Business I Learned from Monopoly.* Philadelphia: Running Press, 2002.

Hopkirk, Peter. *The Great Game: The Struggle for Empire in Central Asia.* Tokyo: Kodansha International, 1992.

Neumann, John von, and Oskar Morgenstern. *Theory of Games and Economic Behavior.* Princeton, NJ: Princeton University Press, 1980.

Chapter 1: The Limits of Loyalty

Bamford, James D., Benjamin Gomes-Casseres, and Michael S. Robinson. *Mastering Alliance Strategy: A Comprehensive Guide to Design, Management, and Organization.* San Francisco: Jossey-Bass, 2002.

Harvard Business School Press. *Harvard Business Review on Strategic Alliances.* Cambridge, MA: Harvard Business School Press, 2002.

Honary, Ehsan. *Total Diplomacy: The Art of Winning RISK.* New York: BookSurge, 2007.

Lynch, Robert P. *Business Alliances Guide: The Hidden Competitive Weapon.* New York: Wiley, 1993.

Chapter 2: The Unlikeliest Go-Between

Axelrod, Alan. *Chronicle of the Indian Wars: From Colonial Times to Wounded Knee.* New York: Macmillan General Reference, 1993.

Bray, John. *The Indian Princess; or, La Belle Sauvage.* New York: Da Capo Press, 1972.

Custis, George W. P. *Pocahontas; or, The Settlers of Virginia.* Philadelphia, 1830.

Davis, John. *Travels of Four Years and a Half in the United States of America during 1798, 1799, 1800, 1801, and 1802*. London: Sold by T. Ostell and H. Caritat for R. Edwards, printer, Bristol, 1803.

Gallay, Alan. *Colonial Wars of North America 1512–1763*. New York: Garland, 1996.

Kohn, George C. *Dictionary of Wars*, New York: Facts on File, 1986.

Phillips, Charles, and Alan Axelrod. *Encyclopedia of Wars*. New York: Facts on File, 2004.

Rountree, Helen C. *Pocahontas, Powhatan, Opechancanough: Three Indian Lives Changed by Jamestown*. Charlottesville: University of Virginia Press, 2006.

Smith, John. *Generall Historie of Virginia, New-England, and the Summer Isles with the Names of the Adventurers, Planters, and Governours from their First Beginning, Ano.1584 to this Present 1624*. London: I. D. and I. H., 1624.

Smith, John. *The True Travels, Adventures and Observations of Captaine Iohn Smith, in Europe, Asia, Africke, and America: Beginning about the Yeere 1593, and Continued to this Present 1629*. Richmond, VA: Franklin Press, 1819.

Waldman, Carl. *Who Was Who in Native American History: Indians and Non-Indians from Early Contacts Through 1900*. New York: Facts on File, 1990.

Williams, William C. *In the American Grain*. Norfolk, CT: New Directions, 1939.

Young, Philip. *Three Bags Full: Essays in American Fiction*. New York: Harcourt Brace Jovanovich, 1972.

Chapter 3: Gilbert and Sullivan

Ainger, Michael. *Gilbert and Sullivan: A Dual Biography*. New York: Oxford University Press, 2002.

Wren, Gayden. *A Most Ingenious Paradox: The Art of Gilbert and Sullivan*. New York: Oxford University Press, 2006.

Chapter 4: The Brothers Wright

Combs, Harry, with Martin Caidin. *Kill Devil Hill: Discovering the Secret of the Wright Brothers*. Boston: Houghton Mifflin, 1979.

Crouch, Tom. *The Bishop's Boys: A Life of Wilbur and Orville Wright*. New York: W. W. Norton, 1989.

Howard, Fred. *Wilbur and Orville: A Biography of the Wright Brothers*. New York: Knopf, 1987.

Chapter 5: The Best of Enemies

Bullock, Alan. *Hitler and Stalin: Parallel Lives*. New York: Vintage Books, 1993.

Churchill, Winston. *The Second World War*. Boston: Houghton Mifflin, 1948–53.

Leonard, Wolfgang. *Betrayal: The Hitler-Stalin Pact of 1939*. New York: St. Martin's Press, 1989.

Overy, Richard. *The Dictators: Hitler's Germany, Stalin's Russia*. New York: W. W. Norton, 2004.

Service, Robert. *Stalin: A Biography*. London: Picador, 2005.

Chapter 6: The Best of Allies

Axelrod, Alan. *Nothing to Fear: Lessons in Leadership from FDR*. New York: Portfolio, 2003.

Churchill, Winston S. *The Grand Alliance* (The Second World War, Vol. 3). Boston: Houghton Mifflin, 1950.

Clodfelter, Micheal. *Warfare and Armed Conflicts: A Statistical Reference to Casualty and Other Figures, 1618–1991*. Jefferson, NC: McFarland, 1992.

Freidel, Frank. *Franklin D. Roosevelt: A Rendezvous with Destiny*. Boston: Little, Brown, 1990.

Kimball, Warren F. *Forged in War: Roosevelt, Churchill, and the Second World War*. Chicago: Ivan R. Dee, 2003.

Leuchtenburg, William E. Franklin D. *Roosevelt and the New Deal: 1932–1940.* New York: Harper & Row, 1963.

Meacham, Jon. *Franklin and Winston: An Intimate Portrait of an Epic Friendship.* New York: Random House, 2003.

Roosevelt, Franklin D. *Memorandum of trip to meet Winston Churchill.* Hyde Park, NY: Franklin D. Roosevelt Presidential Library and Museum. August 23, 1941.

Chapter 7: Ike and the Admiral

Chandler, Alfred D., ed. *The Papers of Dwight David Eisenhower: The War Years II.* Baltimore: Johns Hopkins University Press, 1970.

D'Este, Carlo. *Eisenhower: A Soldier's Life.* New York: Henry Holt, 2002.

Eisenhower, Dwight D. *Crusade in Europe.* Garden City, NY: Doubleday, 1948.

Perret, Geoffrey. *Eisenhower.* Holbrook, MA: Adams Media, 1999.

Chapter 8: The General and the Physicist

Groves, Leslie R. *Now It Can Be Told: The Story of the Manhattan Project.* New York: Da Capo Press, 1983.

Norris, Robert S. *Racing for the Bomb: General Leslie R. Groves, the Manhattan Project's Indispensable Man.* South Royalton, VT: Steerforth Press, 2002.

Rhodes, Richard. *The Making of the Atomic Bomb.* New York: Simon & Schuster, 1986.

Chapter 9: The Tito Factor

Barnett, Neil. *Tito.* London: Haus Publishers Ltd., 2006.

Service, Robert. *Stalin: A Biography.* London: Picador, 2005.

Tucker, Spencer C. *The European Powers in the First World War: An Encyclopedia.* New York: Garland, 1996.

Chapter 10: 41 and 42

Baker, Peter, and Alan Cooperman. "Bush Puts Father, Clinton to Work: Former Presidents to Lead 'Massive' Fundraising Drive." *The Washington Post.* January 4, 2005. http://www.washingtonpost.com/wp-dyn/articles/A44260-2005Jan3.html. June 4, 2008.

"Clinton, Bush: Tsunami Aid Helping." *CBS News Online.* February 21, 2005. http://www.cbsnews.com/stories/2005/02/21/earlyshow/main675227.shtml. June 4, 2008.

"President and Presidents Clinton, Bush Discuss Tsunami Relief Efforts." *The White House Online.* March 8, 2005. http://www.whitehouse.gov/news/releases/2005/03/20050308-9.html. June 4, 2008.

INDEX

PICTURE CREDITS

Courtesy HASBRO: Chapter 1. HASBRO and its logo and RISK are trademarks of Hasbro and are used with permission. © 2008 Hasbro. All rights reserved.

Courtesy of Prints & Photographs Division, Library of Congress: Chapter 2: LC-DIG-pga-03285; Chapter 3: LC-USZC4-7391; Chapter 4: LC-DIG-ppprs-00626;

Courtesy of Wikimedia Commons: Chapter 8: Groves Oppenheimer/Department of Energy

Courtesy The Granger Collection: Chapter 9: The Granger Collection

Courtesy Getty Images: Chapter 10: AFP/Getty Images

Courtesy the National Archives, Washington, D.C.: Chapter 5: 540196; Chapter 6: 111-SC-260486; Chapter 7: Negotiations at Algiers;